Beabull
Complete Owners Manual

Beabull book for care,
costs, feeding, grooming,
health and training.

by

George Hoppendale

and

Asia Moore

Table of Contents

Table of Contents 3

About the Authors 4

Chapter 1: Introduction...5

Chapter 2: The Beabull Hybrid 6

Chapter 3: Choosing a Breeder..19

Chapter 4: Vital Statistics 23

Chapter 5: Temperament 28

Chapter 6: Before You Buy 31

Chapter 7: Choosing the Right Dog.......................................34

Chapter 8: Health Problems...59

Chapter 9: Daily Feeding and Care 70

Chapter 10: House Training 87

Chapter 11: Medical Care & Safety.......................................96

Chapter 12: Grooming...120

Chapter 13: Socializing 134

Chapter 14: Training..140

Chapter 15: Poisonous Foods & Plants 164

Chapter 16: Caring for Aging Dogs.....................................174

Chapter 17: Rescue Organizations.......................................183

Chapter 18: Resources & References 184

About the Authors

George Hoppendale is an experienced writer and a true animal lover. He enjoys writing animal books and advising others about how to take care of their animals to give them a happy home.

Asia Moore is an animal lover, professional Dog Whisperer and experienced Author who has shared her life with many dogs and written more than 350 breed specific books.

Asia lives on Vancouver Island, off the west coast of British Columbia, in Canada, and believes that with the right training, all humans and dogs can live together in harmony.

She and her husband, Jim, teach dog psychology to individuals and groups, and offer canine matchmaking services to humans around the world for those thinking about sharing their life with a dog, in order to help guardians find the right match. They have also dedicated an entire website to their last dog (Boris), who was an amazing part of their dog whispering team for 15 years.

Asia, Jim and Boris also train humans and rehabilitate canines that have developed behavioral issues by teaching dog psychology to human guardians, in order to prevent or help alleviate problem behaviors that arise through common (and often unusual) misunderstandings between humans and their canine counterparts, so that everyone can live a happy and stress-free life together.

Visit Asia & Boris online at the following locations:
www.K-9SuperHeroesDogWhispering.com
www.MustHavePublishing.com
www.KnowsToNose.com
www.AskBoris.com

Chapter 1: Introduction

It's important to gather as much information as possible before you take the plunge to share your home with a furry friend. While humans and dogs have been relying on one another for more than 30,000 years, it's very important that you choose the canine companion that is best suited to your particular lifestyle.

The Beabull Complete Owner's Manual will answer the questions you may have when researching this canine that is part Beagle and part English Bulldog. Learn all about this loyal and curious dog, including facts and secrets, and how to care for every stage of this dog's life.

You will learn about transitioning through house breaking, adolescence, daily care, health problems inherent in the breed, feeding, grooming, training, first commands and beginner hand signals as well as the end of their life, so that you can make an educated decision when deciding whether or not the Beabull designer dog is the breed for you and your family.

Please keep in mind, when reading this book, that it contains generalizations that hold true for most breeds, plus a great deal of highly valuable dog whispering techniques that have been honed and perfected from over 40 years experience while working with a wide variety of canine breeds and other animals in the wild.

While it can be fun and interesting to hear about the ancient history of a breed or about particular inherited traits, or what celebrity may have owned one, I hope you realize the value inherent in all the many positive tips, tricks and dog whispering expertise this book contains.

All of the dog whispering knowledge shared with you within the covers of this book can easily be applied to any breed of canine, because no matter what size, shape, color, purebred or hybrid pedigree may be involved, in order for every dog to be a happy and well-balanced member of your family, it's vital that they receive the right information and energy from their humans so that they can get a started off on the right paw.

^..^ Asia

Chapter 2: The Beabull Hybrid

The *"Beabull"* designer canine will usually have a head that looks more like a Beagle with a longer nose and long ears, attached to a barrel-shaped body that looks more like a Bulldog. This hybrid will often retain some of the Bulldog face wrinkles, and could be classified as a playful and loving and loyal family companion.

This even-tempered dog is a cross between the Beagle and the English Bulldog, where one parent is classified as a purebred scent hound and the other parent is classified as a purebred non-sporting breed.

This mild-mannered, patient and versatile hybrid is adaptable and could be best suited for families with children who are more laid back or for those who like to lead a more energetic lifestyle.

It can also be common practice for those intentionally breeding a mixed canine to breed multi-generational offspring where a 50% Beagle and a 50% English Bulldog (F2 generation) will be bred back to another Beabull in order to attempt to establish a more uniform look.

As the Beagle is small-sized hound and the English Bulldog is a medium-sized dog, the crossing of these two purebreds will usually result in a medium-sized Beabull.

The strong and solid Beabull may have a more slim appearance, like their Beagle parent, or a definitely stocky appearance, like their Bulldog parent. is believed to be a devoted and loving companion that will be affectionate, patient and tolerant of even the most curious children. Usually mild-mannered, like their Bulldog parent, they will switch between bouts of laziness and burst of activity and will enjoy playing games that challenge them mentally.

When two purebred canines are bred together, in the past they were simply referred to as *"mutts"*. Now, when two separate breeds are intentionally crossed or mixed together, they are often referred to as *"designer"* or *"hybrid"* dogs.

The most obvious mark of a *"designer"* or *"hybrid"* dog' is that the resulting puppies are named with what is referred to as a *"portmanteau"* word, which is a word that is a combination of two or more words, syllables or sounds that have been taken from the names of the two or more purebred parents, that becomes the new name of the designer breed.

The term "hybrid" or *"designer dog"* began during the late 20th century, when breeders first began to intentionally mix "Poodles" with other types of purebred canines with the intent of creating offspring that would retain the hypoallergenic "Poodle" coat, as well as traits considered desirable from other popular breeds.

Therefore, in order to better understand this hybrid dog, we need to first consider the traits of both breeds separately.

Although cross breed dogs are not recognized by purebred registries, such as the American Kennel Club (AKC), they are recognized by the International Designer Breed Registry and the American Canine Hybrid Club, where the Beabull designer dog is generally considered to be a medium-sized, athletic, fun-loving, and easy to train companion breed.

When purchasing a hybrid or designer breed canine, you need to keep in mind that while purebred dogs have been carefully bred for many generations to be recognizable by their consistently uniform look, size and temperament, puppies that are produced from combining one breed with another, such as in the case of the Springer Spaniel and Labrador Retriever, may not inherit the same consistent traits from the breeding parents.

This means that puppies born in the same litter can have an appearance that is remarkably different from each of their other siblings, and it can also mean that each litter produced by this type of pairing may be entirely unique.

The original intent may have been to produce a dog that resembled the sturdy Bulldog, but without all the breathing problems, and in most cases that's what you'll get when you breed these two together, it is always possible that there will be a large range of looks and colors produced.

No matter which side of the parenting combination the puppies take after, the Beabull will definitely be a loving, playful and intelligent dog who will enjoy fitting in with whatever their human family has in store for them and whatever activity their guardian has the time to teach.

Before we put these two purebred canines together in one dog, it will be useful to anyone thinking about sharing their life with this hybrid to learn a little bit about both the Beagle and English Bulldog, as this will provide a better understanding of what this mixed breed will usually be like.

1. Beagle

The affectionate and excitable *"Beagle"* is a friendly and sociable, medium to high energy, purebred scent hound that is a member of the Hound Group.

The *"Beagle"* is a small to medium-sized purebred canine that is a member of the hound dog category. The Beagle with their white tipped, stiffly waving flag of a tail, are reminiscent of the larger foxhound, except that they have shorter legs and longer ears.

As a result of their very strong sense of smell, they can tend to be very single minded when they catch a scent.

During a 13-year study, part of which was to determine which breed had the best sense of smell, the Beagle was able to locate the hunted object (a mouse) almost 14 times faster than their closest competitor (the Fox Terrier).

In today's modern world, because of the Beagle's superior sense of smell, they are often employed as a detection dogs, particularly with the United States Department of Agriculture *"Beagle Brigade"* where these smaller hounds are used to sniff out food items in luggage. The Beagle has an average of 220 million scent receptors, as opposed to Man who only has 5 million as well as many other canine breeds who have about half the number as the Beagle.

In Australia, the versatile Beagle is used as a sniffer dog to detect termite infestations, while their smaller, unimposing size makes them also valued therapy dogs. The muscular, yet gentle and friendly Beagle is an intelligent, even-tempered dog that can easily become distracted by their very sensitive nose.

Interestingly, the Beagle is more popular in Canada and the US than in their native Great Britain, and as a result of their gentle dispositions, this breed is often a favorite family pet.

When measured at the shoulder, the Beagle will usually stand between 13 and 16 inches (33 and 41 centimeters) and weigh between 20 and 25 pounds (9 and 11 kilograms) or more, depending on the size of both parents.

The Beagle will be friendly high-energy dog that will love to run and play and will excel at whatever activity their guardian has the time to teach.

Perhaps the most endearing feature of the Beagle is their large, dark, pleading eyes that could melt the heart of the most stoic, and which is also a reason why many of these dogs end up being overweight, as humans have great difficulty resisting the pleading stare when there is any food involved.

The Beagle is an all round versatile dog that also has great stamina and determination, especially when engaged in any sort of hunting activity. At times they can be difficult to train as they easily become distracted by smells.

History: While most canine breeds have shrunk in size, the earliest Beagle was apparently much smaller than our modern day Beagle. Exactly opposite to what has happened to so many older breeds, the Beagle has been bred larger.

This canine used to be known as a *"Pocket Beagle"* or *"Miniature Beagle"* (now extinct) that was approximately 8 or 9 inches (20.32 or 22.86 centimeters) high at the shoulder, which would have meant that they were indeed small enough to carry about in a pocket, has been bred larger.

During the reign of Queen Elizabeth I, she kept many of the now extinct, smaller *"Pocket Beagles"* that would fit into a pocket or saddlebag to ride along during a hunt. Once the larger hounds had located the prey, the smaller, pocket Beagles would continue the chase through dense underbrush.

Queen Elizabeth I called these smaller hounds her *"singing Beagles"* and they were permitted special privileges that sometimes involved entertaining her royal guests by allowing these small hounds to frolic across the plates and cups on the royal dining table.

After breeding Pocket Beagles with larger hunting hounds, the size of the breed gradually changed into the larger form we recognize today as the Beagle.

The modern day Beagle is descended from a mix of several breeds, including the North Country Beagle, the Southern Hound and the Talbot Hound. Some also believe that it is possible that the Beagle may contain some DNA from the Harrier breed, which resembles an English Fox Hound.

As well, very early ancestors of the Beagle can be traced as far back as 5th century ancient Greece. During the time when hunting was an all day pastime, the Beagle was a favorite small hound primarily developed for hunting hare, which was referred to as *"beagling"*.

This small to medium-sized, excitable and loving canine was originally a working scent hound bred and developed in Great Britain during the 1830's for field tracking of both small and larger game, such as rabbits, hares and deer.

The Beagle is a merry, social and enthusiastic dog that enjoys being in the midst of a large pack of dogs or spending time in a large family.

Temperament: One of the reasons the Beagle is such a popular family canine breed is because they are gentle with children, however, they are definitely pack oriented, which means that they can suffer from anxiety if expected to spend many lonely hours without the company and direction of their human guardian.

A Beagle left alone for many long hours may develop barking, baying or howling tendencies, and they may also bay or howl when they catch an interesting scent.

A Beagle is certainly going to be an energetic, fun loving, happy dog with great stamina that lives to run and play, however, you need to keep in mind that this dog, when not trained properly at a young age, can become very vocal. Often these dogs end up in shelters and rescue facilities because the neighbors complain about the noise when this dog is left alone.

Most Beagles are sturdy, yet gentle dogs that are great for children of all ages. They will be alert and faithful companions always eager for the next adventure.

Remember that this dog is a natural scent hound, which means that they could have a high prey drive, and if not well trained and given the opportunity, they may take off after an interesting scent, such as rabbits, cats or even deer.

This breed will become very attached and devoted to its family members, and they will not usually be aggressive toward strangers or other dogs unless they have not been properly socialized at a young age.

This is an alert, intelligent, affectionate, energetic, fun-loving, clever and sometimes distracted dog that will not only enjoy plenty of exercising, this will be essential to their health. The Beagle will be an active dog that is an impressive jumper, climber, and intuitive problem solver who will excel at any activity you have the time to engage in.

If you neglect this dog and do not provide them with regular daily exercise and mental stimulation, they will create their own entertainment, which could include destroying your property or barking to excess.

The Beagle will be a good family dog that is affectionate and totally devoted to the family and while they may not be a particularly good guard dog because they are very friendly to most everyone, they will be good watch dogs who will alert you when someone is approaching.

First recognized by the American Kennel Club in 1885, according to American Kennel Club (AKC) registrations, the Beagle holds the #7 popularity position amongst the 194 registered breeds.

2. English Bulldog

The docile English Bulldog is a short-faced, thick-set, medium-sized purebred canine that is a member of the Non-Sporting Group.

The English Bulldog is easily recognized as a heavy, muscular dog with a distinctively wrinkled face and short nose, often displaying teeth in a prominent under bite.

This friendly, patient dog has short ears, a wide head and shoulders tapering to narrower hips and a corkscrew tail. The stocky Bulldog stands between 12 and 16 inches (30.48 and 40.64 centimeters) at the shoulder and can weigh between 40 and 50 pounds (18 and 22 kilograms) or more.

The Bulldog of today, although still retaining their tough look, is unable to perform the job it was originally created for many hundreds of years ago, as the current Bulldog is unable to grip with their shortened muzzle and they cannot withstand long periods of exercise, especially during warmer weather.

As puppies, the English Bulldog is playful and frisky, however, as an adult they are usually quiet and sedentary, often content to spend the day snoring on the couch.

This is a dog that can be very strong willed and tenacious, which means that when they decide to do something they will usually succeed before you have the time or will to change their mind.

The Bulldog coat is short and straight and while they will shed heavily twice a year, they will also shed all year round. This shorthaired canine is an indoor dog that overheats quickly in the summer and can just as quickly chill in colder weather.

This is a snorting, drooling, wheezing, gassy dog with breathing difficulties that should not be exercised during hot or humid weather because they will have difficulty maintaining the correct body temperature. This is a dog that will prefer living in an air-conditioned home.

A English Bulldog that receives no regular exercise will become obese, which will usually shorten their life, not to mention that extreme boredom can lead to destructive behavior.

This is a dog that may win the prize for the most excessive slobbering and drooling, especially after drinking or eating and when they shake their heads, run for cover, because the slimy saliva will be sprayed all over you, your furniture and up your walls. Many *"slobber"* towels are a must in homes where Bulldogs live.

History: The Bulldog is an ancient breed of canine that has been mentioned in literature as far back at the 1500's and at one time almost became extinct.

Some historians believe that the original Bulldog breed came about by crossbreeding the smaller Pug with the very large Mastiff, while still others believe that the Bulldog and the Mastiff shared genes with the ancient breed known as the "Alaunt", which was a large, Mastiff-like, working breed used to herd oxen and keep them confined in their stalls.

Originally this dog would have been bred for their fierce and courageous temperament because they were used for sporting entertainment in both dog fighting and bull bating competitions, before these cruel practices were banned.

There was a time when the English Bulldog was so savage and ferocious that they would be almost impervious to the pain inflicted upon them during these so-called sporting events, and would fight entirely without concern to themselves.

In bull bating competitions, a bull would be tethered in a ring and the first Bulldog to grab the bull by the nose and wrestle it to the ground would be declared the winner, hence the name "Bulldog". Many English Bulldogs would be maimed or killed during these events.

Thankfully, these cruel sports, such as bull baiting and dog fighting became illegal in 1835, which for the Bulldog breed that was bred specifically for these cruel sporting purposes, meant that the continuation of the breed was placed at jeopardy.

The Bulldog breed was only preserved as a result of several individuals who worked hard at ensuring that this dog did not pass quietly into anonymity.

Those determined to preserve the English Bulldog now realized that it was no longer desirable to retain the previous ferocious qualities of the breed and instead, set about to systematically eliminate the undesirable qualities of this dog's temperament by focusing their efforts solely on improving what they considered to be the breed's finer qualities.

As a result, careful breeding practices carried out over several generations created an English Bulldog that retained the desired physical form without the frightening temperament of the previous ferocious fighter.

Over time, the original Bulldog was crossed with the Pug, which created a Bulldog with a wider, shorter skull. It was during this time that the Bulldog became more of a specimen to be formed and proudly exhibited in the show ring than a dog bred for enduring health or longevity.

At some point in the Bulldog's history it became more fashionable to breed for a certain look, despite compromising the most basic of the dog's functions.

Today, the sweet and gentle English Bulldog has become synonymous for so much that gives the "show-only" world a bad reputation. Whereas, many dog breeds are carefully preserved to retain only the best and healthiest qualities, the English Bulldog has sadly been bred without regard to the dog's own welfare.

Unfortunately, rather than breeding for soundness, many Bulldogs are bred for fashion, and as a result the breed must suffer the consequences of a compromised respiratory system, difficulty walking, eye and skin problems, heart failure and a shortened lifespan.

The Bulldog, as we know them today, would not exist but for the intervention of humankind because they have been systematically bred for large heads, wide chests, narrow hips and squashed faces, which means that more than 90% of these dogs must be delivered by cesarean section.

Most Bulldogs cannot naturally breed, because their short legs and wide chest prevent them from getting the job done. This means that females must be artificially inseminated.

There are now many animal welfare advocates who strongly believe that many English Bulldog breeders have taken selective breeding practices too far with this dog, and have seriously compromised a dog that once a substantial and robust companion.

Temperament: While affectionate and gregarious and most usually friendly to everyone, including all ages of children, without proper socialization they may become testy with some other breeds of dogs.

This dog is usually very determined and may become dominant or stubborn and therefore will do best with a strong guardian who knows how to provide rules and boundaries.

While the Bulldog may be enthusiastic, and they are patient and gentle with children, they are also known to be stubborn and willful which means that they may not be particularly willing or easy to train.

The English Bulldog also has a reputation for being food motivated which can lead to guarding activity around feeding time. Any guarding tendencies should be eliminated at an early age, otherwise young children may be at risk of harm should they venture near the dog's food bowl.

As well, conscientious guardians will need to carefully oversee the feed bowl and exactly what this dog puts in its mouth to ensure that they do not become overweight.

Some English Bulldogs may be entirely couch potatoes, while other may be more energetic. Whatever the energy level of your Bulldog, they still need to go outside for daily walks so that they do not become overweight and so that they can fulfill natural roaming tendencies.

First recognized by the American Kennel Club in 1886 and according to American Kennel Club (AKC) registrations, despite all their health problems, the English Bulldog holds the #5 popularity position amongst the 194 registered breeds.

3. History/Origin of the Beabull

While determining true origin of a specific breed of canine is always met with a certain degree of controversy and many different theories about who was the first, it is likely that this hybrid was first created in the United States.

As far as energy is concerned, this is a dog that is most likely going to land somewhere in between bursts of playful, rambunctious energy, curious pursuit of small prey, and snoozing on the couch.

Being part mischievous, hyperactive Beagle may mean that this loyal dog could have a finely honed sense of smell and a hunting prey drive to go along with it, which means that he or she may howl, especially if they catch an interesting scent on the wind, or are bored and unhappy from being left alone.

Being part Bulldog may mean that as well as being generally patient, calm and mild-mannered, this dog could have an obstinate, stubborn streak when it comes to learning things that they'd rather accomplish in their own time.

When considering this charming, eager to please and often comical hybrid, you will want to keep in mind that when mixing two purebreds together, while it is often difficult to predict what qualities will surface, this combination will usually produce a loving, friendly and playful companion that needs to be in the company of their humans, and will not be happy if expected to spend many hours in solitary confinement.

As with any hybrid canine, while it is always the hope that the resulting puppies will take on the best traits of both breeds, it would be prudent to keep in mind that it is also entirely possible that they could take on some of the less appealing traits of both breeds.

A relative newcomer to the canine world, strong, medium energy Beabull hybrid can exhibit some headstrong traits, and tendency to rough play with other dogs, which means that their guardian will have to exercise firm rules and boundaries at an early age and teach him or her what is, and what is not acceptable behavior.

4. Beabull Secrets

The name *"Beabull"* is a meshing together of the *"Bea"* of the **Beagle** breed with the *"bull"* of the English <u>Bull</u>dog breed to make up this unusual hybrid dog name.

The affectionate and playful Beabull may also be known as the *"Bullgle,"* the *"Bullie Beagle"*, or simply as the *"Beagle/Bulldog" mix.*

This sturdy and strong hybrid may have the tendency to be mouthy or play bite too aggressively during play sessions and socializing with humans and other dogs. This habit will need to be firmly curtailed when the puppy is young so that it does not become a serious problem later in life.

Now, before we get any further into this book, it's important that you please understand that much of the content written in this book can be applied to EVERY dog, because when it comes right down to it, a dog is a dog no matter what size, shape, colour, price tag or fancy purebred or hybrid name we humans might ascribe to them.

Every dog has a uniquely wonderful set of gifts to share with their human counterparts, if only us humans would listen.

They "tell" us when they are unhappy, when they are bored, when they are under-exercised, yet often we do not pay attention, or we just think they are being badly behaved.

Many humans today are deciding to have dogs, instead of children, and then attempting to manipulate their dogs into being small (or large) fur covered children. This is having a seriously detrimental effect upon the health and behaviour of our canine companions who are often confused.

In order to be the best guardians for our dogs, we humans must have a better understanding of what our dogs need from us, rather than what we need from them, so that they can live in safety and harmony within our human environment.

Sadly, many of us humans are not well equipped to give our dogs what they really need and that is why there are so many homeless, abandoned and frustrated dogs.

As a professional dog whisperer who is challenged with the task of finding amicable solutions for canine/human relationships that have gone bad, once the humans understand what needs to be changed, almost every stressful canine/human relationship can be turned into a happy, forever after.

The sad part is that many humans are simply not willing to really understand the breed they are choosing or do the work and devote the time necessary to ensuring that their dog's needs are met.

Almost all canine problems are a direct result of ignorance or simply unwillingness on the part of the canine guardian to learn what the dog truly needs. Forget about the breed for the moment, because what the dog needs to be a happy and well-balanced family member has nothing to do with size, shape, colour or breed.

First and foremost, our dogs need to be respected for their unique canine qualities. For millennia, dog has been considered *"Man's best friend"*, and in today's society, when we want to do the best by our canine companions and create a harmonious relationship, we humans need to spend more time receiving the proper training so that we humans can learn how Man can be dog's best friend.

A Beabull is a dog and therefore can be "Man's or Woman's best friend" providing that the human guardian gains the knowledge they need in order to create a happy environment for the dog.

That's the biggest *"secret"* because if the human treats the dog well and understands what the dog needs, the dog will be happy and the owner will be happy. This is a universal truth that applies to any dog, whether a hybrid Beabull or any other purebred canine.

For example, it's not possible to write a book specifically about *"How to train a Beabull"* or specifically about what *"The first few days with your Beabull"* will entail, etc., because basic training techniques apply to every dog, and every human/dog relationship will be unique.

For this reason, when referring to daily feeding, care, house training, behavioral training, socializing, etc., although there may be specific reference to points relevant to the Beabull breed, these chapters are NOT written to apply specifically to this hybrid, as much of this information can be applied equally successfully to any dog breed.

We've all heard the phrase that *"dog is man's best friend"*, however, what we humans need to remember is that *"With the proper training, man or woman can learn to be dog's best friend."*

Chapter 3: Choosing a Breeder

1. Locating a Reputable Breeder

Although a good breeder cannot guarantee the lifelong health of any puppy, they should easily be able to provide a prospective Beabull guardian with plenty of information about the health of the puppy's parents.

Prospective guardians should definitely ask the breeder what sort of health tests have been carried out on the parents of a puppy they may be considering purchasing.

For instance, a reputable breeder will have had their breeding dogs tested for hip, thyroid, eye or other problems inherent in the breed and prospective puppy purchasers should always inquire about possible congenital problems the parents or grandparents of the puppy might have, including any premature deaths.

2. Meet the Parents

Meeting the mother and father of your new puppy can tell you a great deal about what the temperament and demeanor of your puppy will likely be when they grow into adulthood.

The puppy's personality or temperament will be a combination of what they experience in the early days of their environment when they are in the breeder's care, the genes inherited from both parents and how their guardians train and socialize them. Visiting the breeder several times, observing the parents, interacting with the puppies and asking plenty of questions will help you to get a true feeling for the sincerity of the breeder.

The early environment provided by the breeder and the parents of the puppies can have a formative impact on how well your puppy will ultimately behave as an adult dog.

3. Questions to Ask a Breeder

Get to know your breeder by asking them why they decided to breed the Beabull and how long they have been breeding. Ask if the breeder will permit you to visit their facility and will they give you a tour?

Ask the breeder if they own both breeding parents, or if they do not, ask if they are familiar with, or have worked closely with both parents of the puppy you may be considering.

Ask how often the breeder allows the females and males to breed and reproduce. Ask if the breeder will allow you to see the other dogs in the kennel and notice whether the kennel is clean, well maintained and animal friendly.

Will the breeder permit you to see other adult dogs, or other puppies that the breeder owns, socialize together?

Pay attention to whether the breeder limits the amount of time that you are permitted to handle the puppies. A reputable breeder will be concerned for the safety and health of all their puppies and will only permit serious buyers to handle the puppies. Check to find out if the breeder is registered or recognized by your local, state or national breed organization.

a) Medical Questions: every reputable breeder will certainly ensure that their puppies have received vaccinations and de-worming specific to the age of the puppies.

Always ask the breeder what shots the puppy has received and when it was last de-wormed and ask for the name of the breeder's veterinarian. If you discover that the breeder has not carried out any of these procedures or they are unable to tell you when the last shots or de-worming was carried out, look elsewhere.

Also ask to see the breeder's veterinarian report on the health of the puppy you may be interested in purchasing, and if they cannot produce this report, look elsewhere.

b) Temperament Questions: you will want to choose a puppy with a friendly, easy going and congenial temperament and your breeder should be able to help you with your selection.

A good breeder will have noticed personality and temperament traits very early on in their puppies and should be able to provide a prospective purchaser with valuable insight concerning each puppy's unique personality.

Also ask the breeder about the temperament and personalities of the puppy's parents and ask what they have done to socialize the puppies.

Ask how old the puppies must be before they can be taken to their new homes. If the breeder is willing to let their puppies go any earlier than 10 weeks of age, they are more interested in making a profit than in the health of their puppies.

Always be certain to ask if a puppy you are interested in has displayed any signs of aggression or fear, because if this is happening at such an early age, you may experience behavioral troubles when the puppy becomes older.

c) Guarantee Questions: a reputable breeder will be interested in the lifelong health and wellbeing of all of their puppies and good breeders will want you to call them should a problem arise at any time during the life of your puppy.

As well, a good breeder will want you to return a puppy or dog to them, if for some reason you are unable to continue to care for it, rather than seeing the dog go to a shelter or rescue facility. If the breeder you are considering does not offer this type of return policy, find one who does, because no ethical breeder would ever permit a puppy from one of his or her litters to end up in a shelter.

d) Return Contract: reputable breeders offer return contracts. They do this to protect their reputation and to also make sure that a puppy they have sold that might display a genetic defect will not have the opportunity to breed and continue to spread the defect, which could weaken the entire breed.

Many breeders also offer return contracts because purchasing a hybrid Beabull puppy from a breeder can be an expensive proposition, and if you find out that the puppy has a worrisome genetic defect, this could cost you a great deal with respect to unexpected veterinarian care. In such cases, most good breeders offer a return policy, and will be happy to give you another puppy.

e) Testimonials: ask the breeder you are considering to provide you with testimonials from some of their previous clients, and then actually contact those people to ask them about their experience with the breeder, and the health and temperament of their Beabull dog. A good breeder has nothing to hide and will be more than happy to provide you with testimonials because their best recommendation is a happy customer.

f) Breeder Reputation: the Internet can be a valuable resource when researching the reputation of a breeder. For instance, you will be able to post on most forums discussing breeders to quickly find out what you need to know from those who have firsthand experience.

Also, be prepared to answer questions the breeder may have for you, because a reputable breeder will want to ask a prospective purchaser their own questions, so that they can satisfy themselves that you are going to be a good caretaker for their puppy.

First, do your homework about the Beabull breed and then carry out as much research as possible about the specific breeder you are considering before making your initial visit to their facility. The more information you have gathered about the breed, and the breeder you are considering and the more information the breeder knows about you, the more successful the match will be.

Chapter 4: Vital Statistics

1. Countries of Origin
England is the country of origin for both the Beagle and the English Bulldog. While it can be difficult to know for certain, it is likely that the first intentional pairing of these two purebreds to create the Beabull hybrid occurred in the United States.

2. Litter Size
While more or less can be born, on average there will be 4 to 6 puppies per litter.

3. Height and Weight
When measured at the shoulder, the Beabull may stand between 12 and 16 inches (30.48 and 40.64 centimeters) and weigh between 30 and 60 pounds (13.6 and 27.2 kilograms) depending on the size of both parents.

4. Temperature & Heart Rate
Temperature: 100.5 to 102.5 degrees Fahrenheit (38.05 to 39.16 Celsius).

Respiratory Rate: 10 to 20 per minute

Pulse: Puppies, 120 to 160 per minute. Adults, 60 to 140 per minute.

Gums: should be pink

5. Lifespan
Depending on their size, the Beabull lifespan will most likely be between 10 and 13 years, with some living even longer.

6. Coat Colors and Types
The Beabull is noted for the long muzzle and ears of the Beagle, with the short legs and tail of the Bulldog.

While the short and coarse, double or single coat will be fairly low maintenance, this dog tends to shed a great deal and will require regular brushing with a firm bristle brush, followed by a damp cloth wipe down to keep them looking their best.

This dog will also usually retain the Bulldog face wrinkles, which will need daily cleaning and drying to prevent skin problems.

Common coat colors for the Beabull include brown, fawn, gold and white, and the coat may be a solid color, tri-colored, mixed with white or brindle patterned.

Eyes – will be medium-sized, oval-shaped and usually dark in color, with a curious expression.

Ears – will be medium-size and pendant-shape with rounded tips.

Tail – will usually be short and stubby (like the Bulldog).

Adult Coats: the adult coat will begin to grow in at approximately 9-months of age. The entire process and complete change over to the adult coat will usually take 3 or 4 months or longer to fully complete.

During this time of coat change over, it will be very important to thoroughly brush out your young dog's coat every day to help remove dead hair, while the new coat grows in and they will require brushing every few days to keep them looking their best.

Defining Features: the most distinctive features of the Beabull breed are their affectionate temperament and endearing expression.

7. Intelligence

Stanley Coren, a professor of psychology at the University of British Columbia, in Vancouver, B.C., Canada, published ***The Intelligence of Dogs*** in 1994. Since then this book has become the standard for rating the particular intelligence of different canine breeds.

Coren's book describes three categories of dog intelligence that includes (1) *instinctive intelligence*; (2) *adaptive intelligence*, and (3) *working and obedience intelligence*...where he indicates, *"Instinctive intelligence refers to a dog's ability to carry out tasks it was bred to perform, such as guarding, herding, hunting, pointing, retrieving, or supplying companionship."* Coren further notes that:

> *"Adaptive intelligence refers to how well a dog is able to solve problems on its own.*

"Working and obedience intelligence refers to how quickly a dog is able to learn from humans."

As the Beabull is a combination of two purebred canines, we need to look at the intelligence of each breed separately to get an idea of what the intelligence is likely going to be for the Beabull hybrid.

According to the findings of Stanley Coren, the Beagle ranks #131 out of a possible 138 in the *"Lowest Degree of Working/Obedience Intelligence"* category.

In other words, if one is to agree with the findings of Stanley Coren, this dog can understand new commands after between 80 and 100 repetitions and will obey first commands only 25% of the time, or worse.

Further, Stanley Coren ranks the English Bulldog #136 out of a possible 138, also in the *"Lowest Degree of Working/Obedience Intelligence"* category, which means that the English Bulldog can understand new commands after between 80 and 100 repetitions and will obey first commands only 25% of the time, or worse.

While the outcome of the pairing of these two purebred canines could mean that the offspring of this pairing might not be the brightest bulb in the box, they are usually eager to please, and with the proper guidance may still be considered intelligent in their own way. Remember that the Bulldog is known for being strong willed independent minded and the Beagle half of this dog was originally designed to work on their own when hunting out in the field.

Please keep in mind that there are always exceptions to every study and a particular breed's degree of intelligence can often be related to their early upbringing and how they are trained.

No matter which side of the parent lineage the intelligence of this canine follows, or whether they land somewhere in the middle, in the case of the Beabull, it is highly likely that this designer dog will be as intelligent, playful and devoted companion.

8. Living Conditions

The Beabull will usually be a medium energy dog with a curious and playful temperament, which means that they may do well in smaller living conditions, such as an apartment or condominium, because once they've had a walk or a burst of play activity, they are happy to laze about the home.

Keep in mind that this is also usually a very people-friendly dog, which means that while they will usually alert you to the arrival of visitors, this dog is not likely going to be a good guard dog because they are social, kind-natured and love people.

While intelligent and willing to please, they also tend to be stubborn and would do best with a patient, experienced guardian that understands the importance of both mental and physical stimulation from disciplined walks and daily exercise so that they maintain a healthy weight and calm temperament.

A full grown Beabull will need to burn off their daily pent-up energy by going for at least two or three good "disciplined" walks of 30 minutes to an hour each beside their human companions every day, plus have an opportunity to run free playing a game of fetch.

In order for this curious and loving dog to be well balanced they will want to be close to their human family, and this means taking your dog everywhere with you, which also helps to socialize and exercise their intelligent brains.

Dogs are pack animals, which means that it is not normal for them to be by themselves. Therefore, leaving them alone for many hours every day with nothing for them to do, will be torture for them that could result in any dog becoming depressed or unhappy or making his or her own entertainment by becoming destructive, extremely noisy or attempting to escape so they can wander the neighborhood.

9. Hybrid Vigor

Remember those stories you used to hear when you were a kid when people talked about dogs and how a *"mutt"* was the best kind?

What you may have heard about *"mutts"* being healthier and making better pets is not just an old wife's tail, because it can actually be quite true.

The term *"hybrid vigor"* (also called Heterosis) is a real phenomenon that occurs in every animal (& plant) species during the first pairing or crossing when two separate species are bred together.

Therefore, although all Beabull dogs may not be a first generation cross between a Beagle and a English Bulldog, those who ARE will likely be healthier and mentally more stable than either of the litter's purebred parents.

When both parents share the same traits, in a purebred line, the offspring they produce will be much more likely to display a disease or health problem common to the breed.

On the other hand, while puppies resulting from breeding two distinctly different purebred canines will usually retain physical attributes common to both parents, the puppies will display characteristics which lie somewhere between the two parents.

With respect to health issues, if only one purebred parent carries a trait or health problem common to the breed, when breeding these two purebreds together, this gene will be recessive in the puppies.

With the birth of each successive generation of puppies, where a Beabull is bred to another Beabull, the hybrid vigor will be lost because the more inbreeding that occurs, the more genes the resulting puppies will share in common with the breed parents, which can result in them being prone to more health issues.

Of course, just because dog is a crossbreed does not guarantee that the puppies produced will be a combination of the best of each of their parents.

Despite how conscientious a breeder may be, the way genetics will combine when two different purebred canines are bred together cannot be exactly controlled.

Chapter 5: Temperament

No matter which side of the family this designer puppy takes after, a Beabull is certainly going to be curious, fun loving, and even-tempered dog that is calm and devoted.

This playful dog will thrive when being the center of the family environment, because they form strong and loyal attachments to their humans and absolutely adore being involved in everything that goes on around them, which includes being patient with children.

Not especially being happy with extended times alone in their own company, the Beabull can be a great choice for singles working at home or families where one person usually stays at home when everyone else is out of the house so they usually have company.

Always keep in mind that if this dog does not receive enough exercise that engages both mind and body, this eager to please canine will quickly become bored, and when this happens, the result will inevitably lead to an overweight dog that may develop unwanted destructive behaviors.

A bored and unhappy Beabull, for instance, could spend hours howling and whining, attempting to escape their confinement, inappropriate chewing or any manner of household destruction.

This is a dog that, despite their docile nature, may still retain a moderately strong prey drive and they may howl when an interesting scent catches their attention. He or she will enjoy outdoors pursuits with their human family and while they will protect their family if the need arises, they usually have a friendly, non-aggressive disposition.

While intelligent and eager to please, this hardy hybrid tends to be stubborn, which means that they may not be the best choice for a first time dog guardian, because a firm hand and much patience, that usually comes with experience, is usually required to keep this dog under control.

Every dog needs the discipline of being walked on leash outside of the home each day, as well as the opportunity for off leash time to run and play fetch or enjoy socializing with other dogs. These sturdy dogs tend to bite too much when playing with their humans or other dogs, which means that this habit will need to be curtailed with a firm yet kind and patient hand early on, so that they do not accidentally harm human hands or get into the habit of playing too aggressively with other dogs.

Often stubborn, the Beabull will be much more attentive during any sort of training session when food rewards are offered as incentive. This sturdy, yet sweet-natured and usually calm dog (once puppy exuberance is under control) could be a good choice for families and children of all ages. They will be faithful companions happy to go for a walk or play a game of fetch or hide and seek.

Remember that this designer dog could have a high prey drive, and if not well trained and given the opportunity, they may take off after birds, rabbits, cats or other small animals.

If you neglect this dog and do not provide them with regular daily exercise and mental stimulation, they will become unhealthily overweight and may create their own entertainment, which could include destroying your home or howling all day.

Remember that the perfect dog is not born that way, but rather is the result of the type of environment in which they are raised. This means the care, love, time, attention, training, and ongoing socializing they receive from their humans.

It is imperative to properly socialize any dog, whether a Chihuahua or a Beabull, however, when you have a breed of dog that is sturdy, easily distracted by scents, and is used to thinking for his or herself, it is absolutely vital that you put in the effort and considerable time to begin socialization at an early age and continue it throughout their life.

When you do take the time you will help to ensure that your puppy grows up to be a sensible and calm adult dog that will take their cues from you, rather than acting on their own in situations that could become serious.

All guardians need to be fully aware that a dog who does NOT receive early and continual socialization throughout their lifetime (even one that is generally friendly with everyone, like the Beabull) may learn to become aggressive when he or she encounters people they don't know, which could include visiting neighborhood children or friends, dogs that he or she doesn't know, or unfamiliar situations.

Beabulls are people-oriented dogs that will closely follow their humans all day long. However, since both of their parent breeds are strong-willed and independent-minded, this hybrid combination may not be the best choice for a first-time dog guardian with no previous experience.

1. Behavior With Children and Pets
Generally speaking, the patient and affectionate Beabull will be a good choice for families with young children, because this dog is usually tolerant of even the most bothersome and curious youngsters.

Once their puppy exuberance is under control, they will also be a good choice for families with older children, or older adults who have the energy, time and mobility required so that they are assured of receiving the daily exercise they need.

This is a dog that can be calm and lazy in the home, interspersed with bouts of excitable energy when out on a walk or socializing with other dogs at a local park. This playful dog will be happiest when involved in mentally stimulating games of fetch or hide and seek, where they have to sniff out an object, that include all of the family. As every dog will be unique, this hybrid's guardian will need to discover which types of games their particular dog might excel at.

2. Is This Dog an Escape Artist?
Both the Beagle and the Bulldog sides of this mixed breed are well known for their strong attachment to their humans and stubborn natures. The Beagle is well known for their highly tuned sense of smell and their hound dog yodel when an interesting scent catches their attention. If this dog is left alone in a back yard, and they can figure out how to escape, you may not find them waiting for you when you return.

This dog should not be left alone or unsupervised outside, even in a securely fenced yard because they may figure out how to escape or at the very least put the entire neighborhood on high alert with their howling if they are bored and feeling separation anxiety.

Of course, all dogs will have a much higher urge to roam before they are spayed or neutered, therefore, early spaying or neutering of a Beabull puppy will go a long way toward helping to curb any wanderlust tendencies that may be a result of raging hormones.

Chapter 6: Before You Buy

No matter what breed you may be considering as a possible candidate for sharing your home and life, this decision should never be entered into lightly.

As with any breed, those who may be considering a Beabull need to carry out research and make sure they have all the facts straight before taking the plunge because there are always many important factors to keep in mind.

1. Beabull Quick Review

The following is a quick review of the top categories to carefully consider before choosing a Beabull as your canine companion.

Overall Temperament: Excellent
Friendliness with Family: Excellent
Friendliness with Strangers: Excellent
Suitability for City or Urban Living: Moderate
Suitability for Country or Rural Living: Excellent
Prey Drive: Medium to High
Guarding Capabilities: Poor
Watch Dog Capabilities: Moderate
Canine Sports – Barn Hunt: Excellent
Grooming Requirements: Moderate
Hypoallergenic: NO, heavy shedding
Exercise Requirements: Moderate

Probably the most important consideration when researching a particular breed of dog to share your life with is your activity level and the exercise requirements of the breed you are considering.

2. Pros of Beabull Ownership

The Beabull has many good qualities to consider, including:

- Sturdy and playful
- Patient, loving and curious
- They love to play fetch or search games
- Mild-mannered, devoted and eager to please

- Good with children of all ages and seniors;
- Good with other dogs and animals;
- This may be a good choice for first time dog guardians.

3. Cons of Beabull Ownership

No matter what breed you choose, there will always be some downsides to carefully consider, including:

- This dog wants to be the center of attention and in close contact with their humans
- They have a tendency to bite during play
- They tend to be stubborn and independent-minded
- Moderate prey drive means they may chase smaller animals and birds;
- They tend to howl when an interesting scent catches their attention or they are bored or experiencing separation anxiety if expected to spend time alone;
- Not a good dog to leave alone for long hours every day because they will become unstable, and bored, which can lead to howling and destructive behavior.
- May not be a good choice for a first-time guardian as they require a firm, patient hand, which is usually the result of experience

If I were considering sharing my life with a Beabull, I would need to carefully consider the following factors:

a) Am I fit and active enough to be able to provide this curious and playful dog with the correct amount of daily exercise and mental stimulation they need to be healthy and happy?

b) Do I have enough time in my day to involve this dog in activities beyond daily walks, such as games of fetch or a canine sport?

c) Do I have the knowledge and patience to correct this sturdy dog's tendency to bite when playing with humans or other dogs?

d) Am I resigned to hauling out the vacuum every day because this dog will shed a LOT and the house will be covered in their hair?

e) Am I able to have this dog at my side throughout my day, so that it does not become bored, noisy or destructive?

f) Am I aware that this dog has a tendency to howl, which means that he or she may not be the best choice for a living situation that has close neighbors?

g) Am I resigned to the fact that this dog may have a moderate to high prey drive and a desire to chase birds or small animals?

If you can honestly answer YES to the above list of questions, then the Beabull may be the dog for you.

Chapter 7: Choosing the Right Dog

1. US Clubs, Registries & Breeders

When wondering where to start your search for purchasing a Beabull puppy in the United States, there are several clubs and registries that will be good starting points, including:

The American Canine Hybrid Club (ACHC) is a hybrid registry service established in 1969.

The Designer Breed Registry is a registry is a worldwide registry for designer and purebred dogs.

Adopt a Pet (online): *"...is North America's largest non-profit pet adoption website. We help over 13,600 animal shelters, humane societies, SPCAs, pet rescue groups, and pet adoption agencies advertise their homeless pets to millions of adopters a month, for free. We're all about getting homeless pets into homes.,."*

Smith's Unparalleled Bullies (Pennsylvania): *"...We are a small family who fell in love with both of these adorable breeds. They are so loving and great with both children and animals. We decided to start Smiths Unparalleled Bullies, allowing us to share these wonderful breeds with you. Our Sires and Dams live with us, our other dogs, pets, and are part of our family..."*

Merry's Bullies (North Carolina): *"...My name is Merry Deely and I am a breeder of a wonderful designer hybrid mix - called Beabulls (1/2 Bulldog 1/2 Beagle), or Beabull Bulls (3/4 Bulldog and 1/4 Beagle)... With this breed you get the great attributes of the Bulldog, and you add the health and heartiness of the popular Beagle..."*

2. UK Clubs, Registries & Breeders

Designer Dogs - The Kennel Club is a registration and information service to help prospective owners find Kennel Club "assured breeders" of both purebreds and cross breeds.

While you may find one to adopt from a shelter, an accidental breeding between a Beagle and an English Bulldog, or you may find a litter for sale on YouTube or through other social networking websites or field magazines, currently there are no official breeders to be found online. There are, however, several marketplace listings, advertising Beabull puppies for sale, including:

Pets 4 Homes (online): is the UK's largest free online pet marketplace, relied upon by more than 7 million people monthly to rehome over 2,700 animals each day.

Free Ads (online): *"...Obviously we think freeads is the best marketplace in the world (let alone the UK) and with 12 million buyers, sellers and businesses each year we must be doing something right..."*

3. Average Prices for Puppies
There may be a wide range of *"average"* pricing for any designer or hybrid dog, with some adoptions or rescues beginning around $300 (£232).

There may be a wide variety of "average" breeder pricing for these designer puppies, depending upon whether the resulting litter was simply an accidental breeding or whether they are from an actual established breeder. At the time of writing this book, prices were ranging between $1,100 and $3,000 (£778 and £2,122), depending on the size of the puppies, coat and eye coloring and the expertise of the particular breeder.

Important Note: the authors of this book have not purchased dogs from all the breeders mentioned in this book, and we do not recommend any particular breeder. Make sure that you thoroughly carry out your own research before purchasing a dog from any breeder. There are many dog breeders trading purely for profit and these often will not be overly concerned about the well being of the dogs they breed.

4. Avoiding Puppy Mills or Farms
As soon as a particular breed of dog becomes popular, they also become particularly susceptible to being bred by disreputable, high profit *"puppy mills"* or *"commercial breeding farms"*.

Often a specific dog breed will quickly gain popularity due to the *"Lassie"* effect, which occurs when a dog is featured in a popular movie. Puppy Mill breeding is especially prevalent with cute, smaller breeds, because it takes less space to mass-produce smaller dogs.

This inhumane and cruel world of canine pregnancy for profit occurs all over the world, and if you are not very careful about where and how you purchase your Beabull puppy, you may unknowingly end up promoting this disreputable practice.

Not only do Puppy Mills seriously contribute to overpopulation, they produce diseases, and genetically flawed puppies that may suffer greatly with behavioral and/or health related problems that will cost their guardians greatly in terms grief and stress and unexpected financial burden associated with veterinarian and behavioral costs, while the puppy's life may be cut prematurely short.

These dogs suffer in ways most of us could never imagine. For instance, most of these poor breeding dogs have never walked on solid ground or felt grass as they are housed in cramped wire cages their entire short lives.

Females are bred continuously until they can no longer produce puppies at which time they are sold to laboratories for experiments, killed or dumped on the side of a road.

Although Puppy Mill puppies are sold in a variety of different venues, pet stores are the main source for selling these unfortunate puppies, who are taken away from their mothers far too young (at 4 to 5 weeks of age) and sold to brokers, who pack them into crates to ship them off to pet stores. Many innocent puppies die during transportation.

Think seriously before buying a puppy from a pet store because almost all puppies found in pet stores (whether or not the employees working there are aware of it) are the result of inhumane puppy mill breeding. If you purchase one of these puppies, you are helping to enable and perpetuate this horribly cruel breeding practice.

Puppy Mill puppies are also sold at flea markets, on the side of the road, at the beach, through newspaper ads and through fancy websites and Internet classifieds.

The only way to put these shameful, commercial businesses out of business is by spreading the word and never buying a puppy from a pet store, or any other advertising medium, unless you have first thoroughly checked them out by visiting the facility in person.

Educate yourself and spread the word to others about Puppy Mills, because this is the first step toward ensuring that yourself and everyone you know are never unknowingly involved in the suffering that is forced upon the breeding dogs and puppies trapped in a puppy mill or mass farming operation.

Since October 1, 2018 amendments to the United Kingdom Animal Welfare Act have introduced long needed changes regarding strict compliance for anyone in the business of selling dogs, and all of these changes will be a very strong deterrent for back yard and puppy mill breeders as well as for those illegally importing dogs across borders.

5. How to Choose the Right Puppy

Choosing the right puppy for your family and your lifestyle is more important than you might imagine. Many people do not give serious enough thought to sharing their home with a new puppy before they actually bring one home.

For instance, many of us choose a puppy solely based on what it looks like, because the breed may currently be popular, because they saw one in a TV movie, or because their family had the same kind of dog when they were growing up. None of these are good reasons.

a) Important Questions: in order to be fair to ourselves, our family and the puppy we choose to share our lives with, we humans need to take a serious look at our life, both as it is today and what we envision it being in the next ten to fifteen years, and then ask ourselves a few important, personal questions, and honestly answer them, before making the commitment to a puppy, including:

1) Do I have the time and patience necessary to devote to a puppy, which will grow into a dog who needs a great deal of attention, training and endless amounts of my devotion?

2) Do I lead a physically active, medium or low intensity life? For instance, am I out jogging the streets daily or climbing mountains or would I rather spend my leisure time on the couch?

3) Do I like to travel a lot? Perhaps a dog small enough to travel in the plane cabin with me is a consideration.

4) Am I a neat freak or do I have allergies? A low or non-shedding breed might make more sense.

5) Do I have a young, growing family that takes up all my spare time and are my children old enough to carefully handle a puppy? A dog needs a lot of time and attention.

6) Am I physically fit and healthy enough to be out there walking a dog two to three times a day, every day, rain or shine (and much more when it's just a puppy or a highly active breed)?

7) Can I afford the food costs and the veterinarian expenses that are part of being a conscientious dog guardian?

8) Is the decision to bring a puppy into my life a family decision, or just for the children, who will quickly lose interest?

9) Have I thoroughly researched the breed I'm interested in, and is it truly compatible with my lifestyle or am I considering this breed because I had a similar dog when I was a child, or just because I like the way it looks?

10) What is the number one reason why I want a dog in my life?

Once you ask yourself these important questions and honestly answer them, you will have a much better understanding of the type of puppy that would be best suited for you and your family, and whether or not, it should be a Beabull.

If you are too busy for a dog, or choose the wrong dog that is not compatible with you or your family's energy and lifestyle, you will inevitably end up with an unhappy dog, which will lead to behavioral issues, which then will lead to an unhappy family and extra expenses to hire a professional to help you reverse unwanted behavioral problems.

If you have absolutely decided that the Beabull is the right dog for you, the following tips will help you to choose the right puppy from the litter.

b) Careful Puppy Selection: although your breeder can often help you with selecting the right puppy for you and your family, you will likely be feeling especially drawn to one puppy over another.

Although there are other considerations, how you feel toward a particular puppy in a litter is also an important part of deciding which pup to bring home.

Beyond your feelings, considering other factors will help improve the odds of you having a positive guardianship experience with your new Beabull puppy. For instance, being a little objective when evaluating each puppy in the litter will help you to make the right choice.

While some people become very emotional when choosing a puppy and will be attracted to those who display extremes in behavior because they want to *"save"* them, it is not a particularly good idea to choose a puppy that may be very shy or frightened in the hope that they may grow into a happy, well-behaved dog.

Some people will delve even further into their emotional desires or needs to *"save"* or *"rescue"* and will choose a particular puppy because it has obvious health or behavioral issues, and because they want to provide it with a chance that they believe the puppy might not otherwise have.

While it is certainly wonderful that we humans have the capacity to raise and care for puppies that may be afflicted with health or behavior problems, it's important that these types of decisions are not undertaken lightly as such challenges can lead you down a path that could be an emotional roller coaster of highs and lows that can cause problems for both canine and human alike.

While many minor behavioral problems can be modified with early training, it's important to be aware that the time and effort needed to do so will be difficult to predict and you should be aware that *"rescuing"* a dog that could grow up to have behavioral problems may require the services of a professional dog whisperer or psychologist.

c) Pick of the Litter: generally speaking, when choosing a puppy out of a litter, look for one that is friendly and outgoing, rather than one who is overly aggressive or fearful.

Taking note of a puppy's social skills, when they are still with their litter mates, will help you to choose the right puppy to take home because puppies who demonstrate good social skills with their litter mates are much more likely to develop into easy going, happy adults who play well with other dogs.

In a social setting where all the puppies can be observed together, make the following observations:

When the puppies are playing, notice which puppies are comfortable both on top and on the bottom when play fighting and wresting with their littermates, and which puppies seem to only like being on top. Puppies who don't mind being on the bottom or who appear to be fine with either position, will usually play well with other dogs when they become adults.

If the puppies have toys to play with, observe which puppies try to keep the toys away from the other puppies and which puppies share. Those who want to hoard the toys and keep all other puppies away may be more aggressive with other dogs over food or treats, or in play where toys are involved as they become older.

Notice which puppies seem to like the company of the other pups and which ones seem to be loners. Puppies who like the company of their littermates are more likely to be interested in the company of other dogs as they mature than anti-social puppies.

Observe the reaction of puppies that get yelped at when they bite or roughhouse with another puppy too hard. Puppies who ease up when another puppy yelps or cries are more likely to respond appropriately when they play too roughly as adults.

Also, check to see if the puppy you are interested in is sociable with people, because if they will not come to you, or display fear to strangers, this may be a problem when they become adults.

Further, always check if the puppy you are interested in is relaxed about being handled, because if they are not, they may become difficult with adults and children during daily interactions, during grooming or visits to the veterinarian's office.

6. How to Check If a Puppy is Healthy

Of course you will want to check if a puppy you are considering taking home is not just emotionally healthy, but also physically healthy.

First, ask to see veterinarian reports from the breeder to satisfy yourself that the puppy is as healthy as possible, and then once you make your decision to share your life with a particular puppy, make an appointment with your own veterinarian for a complete examination.

Before you get to this stage, however, there are a few general signs of good health to be aware of when choosing a healthy puppy from a litter, including the following:

- **Breathing** -- a healthy puppy will breathe quietly, without coughing or sneezing, and there will be no crusting or discharge around their nostrils;
- **Body** -- they will look round and well fed, with an obvious layer of fat over their rib cage;
- **Coat** – a healthy puppy will have a soft coat with no dandruff, dullness, greasiness or bald spots;
- **Energy** -- a well rested puppy will be alert and energetic;
- **Hearing** -- a healthy puppy with good hearing should react if you clap your hands behind their head;
- **Genitals** -- a healthy puppy will not have any sort of discharge visible in or around their genital or anal regions;
- **Mobility** – a healthy puppy will walk and run normally without wobbling, limping or seeming to be weak, stiff or sore; and
- **Vision**: -- a healthy puppy will have bright, clear eyes without crust or discharge and they should notice if a ball is rolled past them within their field of vision.

7. One Beabull, or Two?

While getting two Beabull puppies at once will be twice the fun, it will also be twice the work which means that you will need to be doubly alert and patient, and perhaps also lose even more sleep than you bargained for during the potty training phase.

Every puppy needs your constant attention and guidance, therefore, before taking the plunge, ask yourself if you have the time and energy to provide constant attention and guidance for two little puppies that could be running in opposite directions?

Many humans decide to get two puppies because they want their puppy to have someone to play with. Be careful that one of the reasons for this decision is not based on the fact that the human making this decision might not be the ideal candidate for having one puppy, let alone two.

For instance, if the reason you may be considering two puppies is so that the one puppy will not be alone all day while you are at work, stop right there, because leaving one, two or a dozen puppies alone all day while you are at work is a terrible decision that you will likely very soon regret.

If this is your situation, you should NOT be considering any puppy at this stage of your life, and especially not one as loving and connected to their guardians as a Beabull who will suffer severely by being left alone

Another consideration when thinking about whether or not to get two puppies is that often when they grow up, there may be continual sibling rivalry as each puppy vies for your attention.

It is entirely possible that when the puppies mature, they will no longer get along with each other as well as they once did when they were young puppies.

Further, when you have two puppies growing up together, one will always be the more dominant personality that will take over the other, and this could mean that neither puppy will fully develop their individual personalities.

As well, when you have two puppies or dogs in your life, they generally tend to be less affectionate or interested in their human guardians as they have each other in their own pack of dogs to rely upon. This can mean that they will focus so much on each other that they will bond much less with you, which can make it more difficult to train or convince either that you are the actual leader of the pack.

Each puppy will require your individual attention when it comes time for training, and having two puppies in the picture can make it very difficult for them to concentrate or focus on the job at hand.

For instance, when you are teaching puppy #1 to "Sit" while puppy #2 is trying to bite the tail of puppy #1, your job is going to be much more challenging.

Most professional trainers or psychologists will advise that if you want two puppies, not to get them at the exact same time, from the same litter, so that you have the opportunity to house train and teach basic commands to one puppy before you bring another one into the home.

8. Best Age to Purchase a Puppy

Generally speaking, no puppy, including a Beabull puppy, should be removed from their mother any earlier than 8 weeks of age and leaving them until they are **10 to 16 weeks of age is preferred** because this will give them the extra time to learn important life skills from the mother dog, including eating solid food and grooming.

As well, leaving a puppy amongst their littermates for a longer period of time will help to ensure that they learn socialization skills.

Removing a puppy from the mother and other siblings too early could mean that they will miss out on valuable skills, and may not socialize well with others.

For the first month of a puppy's life they will be on a mother's milk only diet. Once the puppy's teeth begin to appear, they will start to be weaned from mother's milk and by the age of 8 weeks should be completely weaned and eating just puppy food.

Removing a puppy from their mother any earlier than eight weeks could mean they are not fully weaned and they would be much more difficult to feed.

9. Should I Get a Male or Female?

Everyone you ask will have a personal opinion about whether you should get a male or a female of any breed. While you will find just as many humans preferring a male over a female Beabull, if you are a first time dog guardian, there may be a few considerations that can help you to make a more informed decision.

For instance, male dogs tend to want to mark or pee on anything upright (trees, telephone poles, tall grass, a stranger's leg) wherever they are out walking much more than females, however, a dominant female will also pee on three legs in an attempt to mark territory.

A male Beabull, even a housebroken one, may try to lift their leg on furniture when visiting a home where there are other dogs present. When spaying and neutering your dog, the operation is much more invasive when spaying a female than the neutering process required for males.

Some humans pick their dogs based on sex alone because they cannot stop themselves from attributing human characteristics to their chosen dogs, and therefore believe that, for instance, a female dog will have a *"sweeter"* temperament, or a male dog may be more *"independent"*.

Of course, this is complete nonsense, because a dog is a dog, and it can be harmful to your relationship to project human emotions onto them or imagine that they will act like humans just because we are human.

Therefore, the best way to choose your puppy will be to take your time observing the litter when you visit the breeder.

10. The Beabull Shopping List

Before bringing home your new puppy or dog for the first time, there will be a list of items you need to make sure you have on hand, including:

Food – usually the puppy will remain on whatever food they have been fed at the breeder's for at least the first couple of weeks, until they are well settled in their new home, so make sure you ask the breeder what brand to buy.

Food and Water Bowls – make sure they are small enough for a young puppy to get close to so that they can easily eat and drink.

Kennel – when you buy your puppy's hard-sided kennel, make sure that you buy the size that will be appropriate for them when they are fully grown. It must be large enough so that (when fully grown) they can easily stand up and turn around inside it.

Martingale Collar, 2 Leashes and Harness – buy the harness and collar small enough to fit your puppy and buy new collars as they grow larger.

Leashes – you will be able to keep the same leashes as all you will ever need is a four foot (1.22 meters) leash made out of nylon webbing with a light weight clip at the end (do not buy a leash that has a heavy clip on the end as it will be difficult for your puppy to carry around).

Soft Beds – you will need one or two for comfortable sleeping when they are not in their kennel. Make sure that you buy the beds large enough for a full-grown dog.

Canine Shampoo and Conditioner – always choose products that are the correct pH for a dog (never use human products). You will also need a non-slip mat for the sink or bathtub and lots of drying towels.

Finger Tooth Brush –- this is a soft, rubber cap that fits over the human's finger to get the puppy used to having their teeth regularly brushed, then a regular or electric toothbrush (an Oral-B electric is best).

Stiff Bristle Brush for daily grooming.

Puppy Nail Scissors – for trimming their toenails, and a small, medium or large-sized pair of plier style nail clippers for when they are full grown.

One or two Soft Toys – or wait until they come home and let them pick their own toys from the store.

Daily Essentials – Pee Pads, Puppy sized Treats, Poop Bags.

Be sure to take your shopping list with you when you go to your local pet store or boutique, otherwise you may forget critical items.

NOTE: if you do not already have a hairdryer, you will need to get one of these, too, so you can dry your puppy after bath time.

11. Puppy Proofing Your Home

Most puppies will be a curious bundle of energy, eager to explore everything, which means that they will get into everything within their reach.

As a responsible puppy guardian, you will want to provide a safe environment for them, which means eliminating all sources of danger, similar to what you would do for a curious toddler.

Be aware that your puppy will want to touch, sniff, taste, chew, investigate and closely inspect every electrical cord, every closet, every nook and cranny of your home and everything you may have left lying about on the floor.

Power cords can be found in just about every room in the home and to a teething puppy, these may look like irresistible, fun chew toys. Make sure that you tuck all power cords securely out of your puppy's reach or enclose them inside a chew-proof PVC tube.

Kitchen – first of all, there are many human foods that can be harmful to dogs, therefore, your kitchen should always be strictly off limits to your puppy any time you are preparing food. Calmly send them out of the kitchen any time you are in the kitchen, and they will quickly get the idea that this area is off limits to them.

Bathroom – bathroom cupboards and drawers or the side of a bathtub where you may leave your shaving supplies can hold many dangers for a young and curious puppy. Kleenex, cotton swabs, Q-tips, toilet paper, razors, pills, soap or other materials left within your puppy's reach are an easy target that could result in an emergency visit to your veterinarian's office. Family members need to put shampoos, soap, facial products, makeup and accessories out of reach or safely inside a cabinet or drawer.

Bedroom – if you don't keep your shoes, slippers and clothing safely behind doors, you may find that your puppy has claimed them for their new chew toys. Be vigilant about keeping everything in its safe place, including jewelry, hair ties, bills, coins, and other items small enough for them to swallow in containers or drawers, and secure any exposed cords or wires.

If you have children, make sure they understand that, especially while your puppy is going through their teething stage, they must keep their rooms picked up and leave nothing that could cause a choking problem to the puppy lying about on the floor or within their reach.

Living Room – we humans spend many hours in our cozy gathering places to watch movies or play games, and often the living areas of our homes will have many items that are very enticing for a curious and teething puppy, such as books, magazines, pillows, iPods, cell phones, TV remotes and more.

You will want to keep your home free of excess clutter and remain vigilant about straightening up and putting things out of sight that could be tempting to your puppy.

Office – we often spend a great deal of time in our home offices, which means that our puppy will want to be there, too, and they will be curious about all the items an office has to offer, such as cell phones, papers, books, magazines, and electrical cords.

Although your puppy might think that rubber bands or paper clips are fun to play with, allowing these items to be within your puppy's reach could end up being a fatal mistake if your puppy swallows them.

Plants: – can be a very tempting target for your puppy's teeth, so you will want to keep them well out their reach. If you have floor plants, they will need to be moved to a shelf or counter or placed behind a closed door until your curious fur friend grows out of the habit of putting everything in their mouth. Also keep in mind that many common houseplants are poisonous to dogs (discussed in Chapter 15).

Garage and Yard – there are obvious as well as subtle dangers that could seriously harm or even kill a puppy, which can often be found in the garage or yard. Some of these might include antifreeze, gasoline, fertilizers, rat, mice, snail and slug poison, weed killer, paint, cleaners and solvents, grass seed, bark mulch and various insecticides.

If you are storing any of these toxic substances in your garage or garden shed, make certain that you keep all such products inside a locked cabinet, or stored on high shelves that your puppy will not be able to reach. Even better, choose not to use toxic chemicals anywhere in your home or yard.

12. Puppy Hazard Home Inspection

Every conscientious puppy guardian needs to take a serious look around the home not just from the human eye level, but also from the eye level of a Beabull puppy.

This means literally crawling around your floors. This can be a fun exercise to ask your children to help you with.

Your puppy has a much lower vantage point than you do when standing, therefore, there may be items in your environment that could potentially be harmful to a puppy that a human might not notice unless you get down on the floor and take a really good look.

13. First Weeks With Your Puppy

a) The First Night: before you go to the breeder's to pick up your new puppy, vacuum your floors, including all the dust bunnies under the bed.

Do a last minute check of every room to make sure that everything that could be a puppy hazard is carefully tucked away out of sight and that nothing is left on the floor or low down on shelves where a curious puppy might get into trouble. Close most of the doors inside your home, so that there are just one or two rooms that the puppy will have access to.

You have already been shopping and have everything you need, so get out a puppy pee pad and have it at the ready when you bring your new fur friend home.

Also have your soft bed(s) in an area where you will be spending most of your time and where your puppy can easily find them. If you have already purchased a soft toy, take the toy with you when you go to pick up your puppy.

NOTE: take either your hard-sided kennel or your soft-sided "Sherpa" travel bag (lined with pee pads) with you when going to bring your new puppy home, and make sure that it is securely fastened to the seat of your vehicle with the seatbelt restraint system.

Even though you will be tempted to hold your new puppy in your lap on the drive home, this is a very dangerous place for them to be, in case of an accident. Place them inside their kennel or bag, which will be lined with soft towels and perhaps even a warm, towel wrapped hot water bottle (and a pee pad), and close the door.

If you have a friend who can drive for you, sit beside your puppy in the back seat, and if they cry on the way home, remind them that they are not alone with your soft, soothing voice.

Before bringing your new puppy inside your home, take them to the place where you want them to relieve themselves and try to wait it out long enough for them to at least go pee. Then bring them inside your home and introduce them to the area where their food and water bowls will be kept, in case they are hungry or thirsty.

Let your puppy wander around sniffing and checking out their new surroundings and encourage them to follow you wherever you go. Show them where the puppy pee pad is located and place it near the door where you will exit to take them outside to go potty. Many pee pads are scented to encourage a puppy to pee, and if they do, happily praise them.

Show them where their hard-sided kennel is (in your bedroom) and put them inside with the door open while you sit on the floor in front of it and quietly encourage them to relax inside their kennel.

Depending on the time of day when you bring your new puppy home for the first time, practice this kennel exercise several times throughout the day, and if they will take a little treat each time you encourage them to go inside their kennel, this will help to further encourage the behavior of them wanting to go inside.

After they have had their evening meal, take them outside approximately 20 minutes later to go to the bathroom, and when they do, make sure you are very enthusiastic with your praise and perhaps even give a little treat.

So far your puppy has only been allowed in several rooms of your home, as you have kept the other doors closed, so keep it this way for the first few days.

Before it's time for bed, again take your puppy outside for a very short walk to the same place where they last went potty and make sure that they go pee before bringing them back inside.

Before bed, prepare your puppy's hot water bottle and wrap it in a towel so that it will not be too hot for them, and place it inside their hard-sided kennel (in your bedroom).

Turn the lights down low and invite your puppy to go inside their kennel and if they seem interested, perhaps give them a soft toy to have inside with them. Let them walk into the kennel under their own steam and when they do, give them a little treat (if they are interested) and encourage them to snuggle down to sleep while you are sitting on the floor in front of the kennel.

Once they have settled down inside their kennel, close the door, go to your bed and turn all the lights off. It may help your puppy to sleep during their first night home, if you can play quiet, soothing music in the background.

If they start to cry or whine, stay calm and have compassion because this is the first time in their young life when they do not have the comfort of their mother or their litter mates.

Do not let them out of their kennel if they are crying, but rather, simply reassure them with your calm voice that they are not alone until they fall asleep.

TIP: if your bed is wide enough to accommodate your puppy's kennel, it may help them to fall asleep for the first few nights in their new kennel, if you have it beside you on top of the bed, so that you are closer to them. If there is any danger of the kennel falling off the bed during the night, do NOT do this as you will traumatize your puppy and make them afraid of their kennel.

b) The First Week: during the first week, you and your new Beabull puppy will be getting settled into their new routine, which will involve you getting used to your puppy's needs as they also get used to your usual schedule.

Be as consistent as possible with your waking and sleeping routine, getting up and going to bed at the same time each day, so that it will be easier for your puppy to get into the flow and routine of their new life.

First thing in the morning, remove your puppy from their kennel and take them immediately outside to relieve themselves at the place where they last went pee.

At this time, if you are teaching them to ring a doorbell to go outside, let them ring the bell before you go out the door with them, whether you are carrying them, or whether they are walking out the door on their own.

NOTE: during the first week, you may want to carry your puppy outside first thing in the morning as they may not be able to hold it for very long once waking up.

When you bring them back inside, you can let them follow you so they get used to their new leash and/or harness arrangement. Be very careful not to drag your puppy if they stop or pull back on the leash.

TIP: if they refuse to walk on the leash, just hold the tension toward you (without pulling) while encouraging them to walk toward you, until they start to move forward again.

Now it will be time for their first feed of the day, and after they have finished eating, keep an eye on the clock, because you will want to take them outside to relieve themselves in about 20 minutes.

When your puppy is not eating or napping, they will be wanting to explore and have little play sessions with you and these times will help you bond with your puppy more and more each day.

As their new guardian, it will be your responsibility to keep a close eye on them throughout the day, so that you can notice when they need to relieve themselves and either take them to their pee pad or take them outside.

You will also need to make sure that they are eating and drinking enough throughout the day, so set regular feeding times at least three times a day.

Also set specific times in the day when you will take your puppy out for a little walk on leash and harness, so that they are not only going outside when they need to relieve themselves, but they are also learning to explore their new neighborhood with you beside them.

When your Beabull puppy is still very young, you will not want to walk for a long time as they will get tired easily, so keep your walks to no more than 15 or 20 minutes during your first week and if they seem tired or cold, pick them up and carry them home.

14. Common Mistakes to Avoid
a) Sleeping in Your Bed: many humans make the mistake of allowing a

crying puppy to sleep with them in their bed, and while this may help to calm and comfort a new puppy, it will set a dangerous precedent that can result in behavioral problems later in their life. As well, a sleeping human body can easily crush a puppy.

As much as it may pull on your heart strings to hear your new puppy crying the first couple of nights in their kennel, a little tough love at the beginning will keep them safe while helping them to learn to both love and respect you as their leader.

b) Picking Them Up at the Wrong Time: never pick your puppy up if they display nervousness, fear or aggression (such as growling) toward an object, person or other pet, because this will be rewarding them for unbalanced behavior.

Instead, your puppy needs to be gently corrected by you, with firm and calm energy so that they learn not to react with fear or aggression.

c) Armpit Alligators: when your Beabull is a small puppy, be aware that many guardians get into the bad habit of carrying a small dog far too much. They need to be on the ground and walking on their own so that they do not become overly confident because a dog that is carried by their guardian is literally being placed in the *"top dog"* position.

Humans who constantly carry small dogs around rather than allowing them to walk on their own can often inadvertently create what I refer to as an *"armpit alligator"* situation.

This happens when the dog becomes possessive of it's guardian who carries it everywhere, and when another adult, child or dog sees the cute little dog and approaches to say hello, the cute little dog who has been inadvertently trained to believe that it is the boss, may then lunge, snap and/or growl.

d) Playing Too Hard or Too Long: many humans play too hard or allow their children to play too long or too roughly with a young puppy.

You need to remember that a young puppy tires very easily and especially during the critical growing phases of their young life, they need their rest.

e) Hand Play: always discourage your puppy from chewing or biting your hands, or any part of your body for that matter.

If you allow them to do this when they are puppies, they will want to continue to do so when they have strong jaws and adult teeth and this is not acceptable behavior for any breed of dog.

Do not get into the habit of playing the *"hand"* game, where you rough up the puppy and slide them across the floor with your hands, because this will teach your puppy that your hands are playthings and you will have to work hard to break this bad habit.

When your puppy is teething, they will naturally want to chew on everything within reach, and this will include you. As cute as you might think it is, this is not an acceptable behavior and you need to gently, but firmly, discourage the habit.

A light flick with a finger on the end of a puppy nose, combined with a firm "NO" and removing the enticing fingers by making a fist when they are trying to bite human fingers will discourage them from this activity.

f) Not Getting Used to Grooming: not taking the time to get your Beabull used to a regular grooming routine, including bathing, brushing, toenail clipping and teeth brushing can lead to a lifetime of trauma for both human and dog every time these procedures must be performed.

Set aside a few minutes each day for your grooming routine.

NOTE: get your puppy used to being up high, on a table or countertop when you are grooming them, because when it comes time for a full grooming session, or a visit to the vet's office where they will be placed on an examination table, then they will not be stressed by being placed in an unfamiliar situation.

g) Free Feeding: means to keep food in your puppy's bowl 24/7 so that they can eat any time of the day or night, whenever they feel like it.

While free feeding a young puppy can be a good idea (especially with very small dogs) until they are about four or five months old, many guardians often get into the bad habit of allowing their adult dogs to continue to eat food any time they want, by leaving food out 24/7.

This can be a serious mistake, as your dog needs to know that you are absolutely in control of their food.

If your dog does not associate the food they eat with you, they may become picky eaters or think that they are in charge, which can lead to other behavioral issues later in life.

h) Treating Them Like Fur Children: do not get into the bad habit of treating your Beabull like a small fur human, because even though they may try their best to please you, and their doggy smarts could help them to succeed in most instances, not honoring them for the amazing dog they are will only cause them confusion that could lead to behavioral problems.

Remember that the one thing that your dog is the absolute best at is being a dog.

A well-balanced dog thrives on rules and boundaries, and when they understand that there is no question that you are their leader and they are your follower, they will live a contented, happy and stress-free life.

i) Distraction and Replacement: when your puppy tries to chew on your hand, foot, or your clothing, or anything else that is not fair game, you need to firmly and calmly tell them "No", and then distract them by replacing what they are not supposed to be chewing with their chew toy.

Make sure that you happily praise them every time they choose the toy to chew on. If the puppy persists in chewing on you, remove yourself from the equation by getting up and walking away. If they are really persistent, put them inside their kennel with a favorite chew toy until they calm down.

Always praise your puppy when they stop inappropriate behavior or replace inappropriate behavior with something that is acceptable to you, so that they begin to understand what they can and cannot do.

15. Bonding With Your Dog
You will begin bonding with your puppy from the very first moment you bring them home from the breeders.

This is the time when your puppy will be the most upset and nervous, as they will no longer have the guidance, warmth and comfort of their mother or their other littermates, and you will need to take on the role of being your new puppy's center of attention.

Be patient, kind and gentle with them as they are learning you are now their new center of the universe.

Your daily interaction with your puppy during play sessions and especially your disciplined exercises, including going for walks on leash, and teaching commands and tricks, will all be wonderful bonding opportunities.

Do not make the mistake of thinking that *"bonding"* with your new puppy can only happen if you are playing or cuddling together, because the very best bonding happens when you are kindly teaching rules and boundaries, and this intelligent puppy will be most eager to learn.

16. What Does the Wag Mean?

It can be a mistake to automatically assume that if a dog is wagging their tail that they are happy and friendly.

When determining a dog's true intent or demeanor, you need to take into consideration the entire dog because it is entirely possible that a dog can be wagging it's tail just before it decides to take an aggressive lunge toward you.

More important in determining the emotional state of a dog is the height or positioning of the their tail. For instance, a tail that is held parallel to the dog's back usually suggests that the dog is feeling relaxed, whereas, if the tail is held stiffly vertical, this usually means that the dog may be feeling aggressive or dominant.

A tail held much lower can mean that the dog is feeling stressed, afraid, submissive or unwell and if the tail is tucked underneath the dog's body, this is most often a sign that the dog is feeling stressed, fearful or threatened by another dog or person.

Paying attention to your dog's tail can help you to know when you need to step in and make some space between your dog and another more dominant dog.

Of course, different breeds naturally carry their tails at different heights, so you will need to take this into consideration when studying your dog's tail so that you get used to their particular signals.

As well, the speed the tail is moving at will also give you an idea of the mental state of the dog because the speed of the wag usually indicates how excited a dog may be.

For instance, a slow, slightly swinging wag can often mean that the dog is tentative about greeting another dog, and this is more of a questioning type of wag, whereas a fast moving tail held high can mean that a dog is about to challenge or threaten another less dominant dog.

The Beabull may or may not have much of a tail as some will have the short or corkscrew tail of the Bulldog parent.

Interestingly, two veterinarians at the University of Bari and a neuroscientist at the University of Trieste, in Italy, published a paper in which their research outlined that dogs' tails wagged more to their right side when they had positive feelings about a person or situation, and more to the left side when they were feeling negative.

While certainly a dog's tail can help us humans to understand how our dogs might be feeling, there are many other factors to take into consideration when determining your dog's state of mind.

17. What Does the Bark Mean?

Of course, our dogs bark for a wide variety of reasons, and every dog is different, depending upon their natural breed tendencies and how they were raised, and this section discusses some of the more common reasons why a dog might be barking.

a) Communication: since the very first dog, they have communicated over long distances by howling to one another and when in closer proximity, barking to warn off other dogs approaching what they consider to be their territory or in excitement or happiness when greeting another member of the dog pack.

Now, our domesticated dogs have learned that barking for a wide variety of reasons, in a guard dog capacity to alert us to someone approaching the home, in anticipation of their favorite food, when they are afraid or frustrated, or to let us know they want to play is an effective way to get the attention of us humans because barking is a difficult noise to ignore.

b) Danger: of course, our canine companions will bark to alert us to what they believe might be a dangerous situation, but how do we learn to understand the difference between what our dogs perceive as danger and what is truly dangerous, or indeed teach our best friends the difference?

We want our dogs to tell us when there is a real imminent danger and in this case, should the danger involve an unwanted intruder, we want them to bark loudly to possibly scare this threat away.

Unfortunately, many dogs are not quite as discerning as we humans might prefer, and as such they may end up barking during situations that we humans would consider inappropriate or just plain annoying.

When our dogs are barking for a reason we are not yet aware of, we need to calmly assess the situation rather than immediately becoming annoyed. We also need to remember that our dog's sense of smell, hearing and sometimes eyesight is far more acute than our own, so we need to give them an opportunity to tell us they just heard, saw or sensed something that they are worried or uncertain about.

Rather than ignoring our dogs (or yelling at them) when they are attempting to "tell" us that something is bothering them, even if we ourselves understand that the noise the dog just heard is only the neighbor pulling into their driveway, is to calmly acknowledge the dog's concern by saying, *"OK, good boy"* or *"OK, good girl"* and then asking them to come to you. This way you have quietly and calmly let your dog know that the situation is nothing to be concerned about and you have asked them to move away from the target they are concerned about, which will usually stop the barking.

c) **Attention:** many dogs will learn to bark to get their owner's attention, just because they are bored or want to be taken outside for an interesting walk or a trip to the local park to chase a ball. Our canine companions are very good at manipulating us in this way, and if we fall for it, we are setting up an annoying precedent that could plague us for the remainder of our relationship.

When a dog is barking to gain their guardian's attention, even if it is warranted because (in this example) it is certainly time to go out for a walk, we humans must not be immediately manipulated. Instead, we need to calmly ask our dog to do something for us, before leaping up and getting the leash to take our dog out.

After our dog has performed a calm and quiet task for us, such as sit and lie down, then we can decide to take our dog out for a walk.
In another example, often you will see a dog and their guardian at the local dog park playing fetch and when the human is not throwing that ball quickly enough to satisfy the dog's desire to run and fetch, the dog will be madly barking at the human guardian.

Do not make the mistake of allowing your dog to manipulate you in this situation, because if you do, you will have created another bad habit that will very quickly become not just annoying to you, but also annoying to everyone else in the park.

Before throwing a ball or Frisbee, etc., for a dog that loves to retrieve, it is important to always ask the dog to sit and make eye contact with you.

Often the types of canines that are overly exuberant with chasing a ball or Frisbee have learned this barking behavior from their humans who allowed themselves to be literally at the beckon call of the dog, and they did this by throwing the ball every time the dog barked.

If you allow your dog to dictate to you when you will throw the ball, they will quickly learn that barking gets them their desired result, and you have just created an annoying, rude dog who is yelling at you in doggy language to do their bidding. In this type of ball retrieving scenario, the dog has become ball *"obsessed"* and is no longer really paying attention to the guardian's commands, as they are solely focusing on where the ball is.

There are many situations in which a dog may bark to convey a certain message, such as letting you know when they need to go outside for potty, and of course, this is a good thing.

However, in all other situations where a dog is barking to demand attention or an object or food, this is when you need to ask them to do something for you, and then only if you want to give them what they are asking for, do you follow through.

Also, remember to stay calm when a dog is demanding attention because even negative attention can be rewarding for a dog that can then learn further habits that will not be particularly acceptable for the human side of the relationship.

d) Boredom or Separation Anxiety: many dogs, especially those who have not been properly trained or that have not been allowed to understand that they have rules and boundaries, and are treated like children, will bark loudly when left at home alone and they are bored or are feeling the anxiety of being alone.

The Beabull tends to howl, a trait they inherit from their Beagle parent, when they catch an interesting scent on the wind, are feeling bored or stress and anxiety from being left alone.

Many times we humans believe that a dog is barking when being left alone because the dog is experiencing "separation anxiety", when in fact what the dog is really experiencing is the frustration of observing a member of the pack which they believe to be their follower (i.e. You) leaving them and they are loudly verbalizing this frustration and displeasure because, in the dog world, the pack follower does NOT leave the pack leader. In these cases, the humans really need the expert advice of a dog whisperer or dog psychologist to help turn the situation around and put the human guardian back in the driver's seat.

Breaking a dog of the habit of loud barking when they are left alone can be solved in two different ways, with the most obvious being that you simply take your dog with you wherever you go, because after all, they are pack animals, and in order for them to be really happy and well balanced, they need the constant direction of their leader (which is supposed to be you).

The other, much more lengthy and often more time consuming way to solve a barking problem, involves hiring a professional to help assess why the problem has occurred and devise a plan that will work for your unique situation.

e) Fear or Pain: another reason our canine companions will bark is when they are very frightened or in pain and this is usually a type of bark that sounds quite different from all the others, often being a combination of a bark and a whine, or a yelping type of noise.

This is a bark that you will want to pay close attention to so that you can quickly respond and offer the dog assistance that they may need.

Whatever reason your dog may be barking or howling, always remember that this is how they communicate and "tell" us that they want something or are concerned, afraid, nervous or unhappy about something, and as their guardians, we humans need to pay attention.

Chapter 8: Health Problems

When considering what sort of health problems a designer or cross bred dog may be prone to, you will need to first consider the health problems known to be associated with each breed individually and perhaps then pay closer attention to health problems that may be inherent in both breeds.

Next, you will need to take into consideration that if the designer dog is 50% one breed and 50% another that this crossing will provide the puppies with the benefits of what is called "hybrid vigor".

This means that a hybrid puppy will likely benefit physically as well as mentally from having a more varied genetic makeup than a 100% purebred puppy which could be afflicted by or susceptible to health problems that both of the purebred parents may also have.

Generally speaking, while a Beabull puppy may be susceptible to any type of health conditions that affect either of their parents, because this dog is half Beagle and half Bulldog, they may be genetically healthier than either of their purebred parents.

Further, many potential health conditions can be avoided when choosing your puppy from a reputable breeder and then following a careful health care regimen throughout the life of your dog. Health problems inherent in both parent breeds are noted with an asterisk (*).

1. Beagle Health Concerns

While some Beagles may be plagued with a wide number of health problems, others can be much healthier and may live on average 10 to 15 years or longer. Common genetic and other health problems that may afflict this breed include:

01) *Obesity: t**he Beagle is almost as well known for being prone to being overweight, as they are known for their heightened sense of smell. This is a dog that has a voracious appetite and can literally sniff out food a mile away. Obesity can lead to joint problems and heart disease.

02) *Hip Dysplasia: is a condition in which the head of the femur fits improperly into the hip joint socket. Factors that have an influence include nutrition and the weight of the dog. This dog easily suffers from obesity, and a dog's environment and the condition of the hips of its parents can exacerbate the problem. Screening for hip dysplasia is recommended for breeding stock.

03) *Hypothyroidism: is an under-active thyroid condition in which the gland does not produce enough hormone, which can lead to a slower metabolism, which in turn can lead to weight gain, tiredness, delays in growth, and intolerance to cold. Treatment involves thyroid replacement therapy.

04) Dwarfism: in the Beagle can cause a condition called *"funny puppy syndrome"*, in which a puppy develops with a crooked back and weak legs.

05) Glaucoma: this eye disease, which is usually caused by an increase of fluid pressure in the eye, can cause permanent damage to the dog's vision in the affected eye or eyes, which, if left untreated, can lead to blindness.

06) *Cataracts: usually appear between the ages of two and four years and are common in many breeds. This is an eye condition where the lens becomes cloudy or milky, which would be like trying to see through a foggy window. This eye condition can appear from birth to 3 years of age and will usually lead to blindness.

07) Corneal Ulcers: when the clear outer capsule in the dog's eye becomes irritated, scratched or somehow damaged through injury that is left untreated, the area becomes inflamed and bacteria can enter which can then lead to infection which will then cause an ulcer.

A dog suffering from a scratch or an ulcer on the cornea of the eye will be experiencing pain, tearing and itching and often discharge and will often squint and paw at the eye, which can make the problem worse. Treatment will depend upon how severe the ulcer may be and while milder cases will involve applying antibiotic ointments, more severe cases can involve surgery.

08) *Cherry Eye: many breeds can suffer from this genetic eye problem, including the Beagle, where the gland of the third eyelid prolapses or slips in the corner of the eye, as a result of weakness of the connective tissue surrounding the gland, causing a pink fleshy protrusion to extend or bulge over the edge of the dog's eyelid.

It is recommended to take your dog to the veterinarian as soon as you notice this condition because treatment will require pushing the prolapsed gland back into the pocket.

09) *Entropion: is a condition in which the dog's eyelid will roll inward which then causes the lashes to rub against the eyeball. Left untreated, this condition can severely damage the dog's eye, even causing blindness. Surgery is required to correct this problem.

10) Ectropion: in a dog suffering from this condition the lower eyelid will turn outward and requires surgery to repair.

11) Retinal Dysplasia: this eye disease appears as streaks or dots in the retina of the dog's eye, which can lead to blindness.

12) Epiphoria (wet eye): is an overflowing of tears or excessive tearing that can occur when a dog's tear ducts do not drain properly, or drain excessively. Infections, allergies and other eye issues can also cause this problem.

Treatment will depend on the cause, and may include removal of a foreign object and the application of an anti-inflammatory eye ointment. For breeds prone to this problem, wiping the area around the eye with warm water or a saline solution may be all that is required. If the problem is caused by an allergen, your vet may prescribe mild eye drops.

13) Otitis Externa: is an inflammation of the ear canal, which can become chronic, and causes discomfort, irritation and pain. Ear infections are common due to their long, floppy ears, which prevents the inner ear from receiving enough airflow to keep the ears dry.

14) Cerebellar Cortical Degeneration: a puppy affected by this rare disease will have trouble with coordination, causing them to move slower, fall often or have an irregular gait. There is a genetic test available to rule out this type of degeneration, which affects 0.1% of dogs.

15) Immune Mediated Polygenic Arthritis: is another rare condition caused when the Beagle's immune system attacks the dog's joints, which can occur at a young age. Steroid treatments can sometimes be effective in alleviating symptoms.

16) *Reverse Sneezing (Brachycephalic Syndrome): this phenomenon, more often seen in short-nosed (brachycephalic) breeds of dogs, can also affect the Beagle. A dog having a reverse sneezing episode will often make a sound that sounds like goose honking, which is a rapid drawing of air in through the nose and mouth. This can occur for a variety of reasons, such as over-excitement, exercising in hot weather or irritants in the air causing sinus irritation. Episodes usually only last a few seconds with no apparent ill effects to the dog.

17) Epilepsy: most epileptic seizures can be controlled medically. However, it is very important to have a Beagle immediately diagnosed by a veterinarian if seizures begin so that the severity of the condition can be properly assessed.

18) Chinese Beagle Syndrome (CBS): is an abnormal growth of the dog's skull that grows wider than normal and creates slanted eyes. Otherwise, the growth of the dog is normal, however, dogs with CBS often will also have abnormal toes and heart problems. There is no DNA test for this usually rare syndrome.

19) Diabetes: is one of the most common canine hormonal diseases that can occur at quite an early age (18-months) but may not be diagnosed until much later in the dog's life, between 7 and 10 years of age. Interestingly, 70% of diabetes is seen in female dogs.

Usually the first signs of this disease is a normal appetite, with an increased consumption of water and weight loss. Also, the sudden onset of cataracts may indicate an underlying diabetes cause. Diabetes, just as it is in humans, is a treatable condition in our canine counterparts requiring insulin injections to return the blood sugar levels to an acceptable level.

20) Ear Infections: as a result of their long hanging ears, this dog is commonly prone to ear infection or inflammation, therefore, guardians need to make sure that the ears are kept clean, dry and free of excessive hair growth.

21) Intervertebral Disc Disease: the intervertebral disks function to cushion the spine, and if they bulge or rupture, can cause nerve problems as well as loss of coordination and severe pain. If this problem is not treated, it can result in permanent weakness or paralysis.

22) *Bloat: is a life-threatening, common occurrence that can affect any deep-chested canine, such as the Bulldog, and 50% of dogs that develop bloat do not survive. This condition can happen very quickly, especially if you feed your dog right after vigorous exercise, or if they are a very fast eater and gulp in large quantities of air with their food.
Bloat is a serious, life-threatening condition that requires immediate veterinary intervention. If you have a deep chested dog that tends to gulp their food, get them a slow feeder type of bowl to slow down their eating

process and never feed them immediately after exercise or having had a large drink of water.

Bloat is a serious, life-threatening condition that requires immediate veterinary intervention. If you have a deep chested dog that tends to gulp their food, get them a slow feeder type of bowl to slow down their eating process and never feed them immediately after exercise or having had a large drink of water.

2. Bulldog Health Concerns

While a healthy Bulldog may live to be 8 to 10 years or more, this dog is known to suffer from many health conditions, including:

01) *Hip and Elbow Dysplasia: is a condition in which the head of the femur fits improperly into the hip or elbow joint socket. Factors that have an influence include nutrition and the weight of the dog. As this is a heavy dog that also easily suffers from obesity, a dog's environment and the condition of the hips and elbows of its parents can exacerbate the problem. Screening for hip and elbow dysplasia is recommended for breeding stock.

02) Elbow Subluxation: is a condition caused when the joint of the dog's elbow is loose and as a result falls out of alignment.

03) *Brachycephalic Syndrome (Reverse Sneezing): occurs in short-nosed breeds, such as the Bulldog. When they get excited from exercise or anticipating a favorite treat, they are prone to a condition that creates a goose honking sound, which causes them to hang their head, gasp and snort.

This condition is caused when fluid (water or saliva) or debris gets traps underneath the dog's palate, which then irritates the throat and creates a breathing problem.

Although reverse sneezing episodes often sound alarming, they are not usually harmful and pass quickly. It can be helpful to calm the dog, gently rub their throat or cover their nose, or apply a light, sharp squeeze around the ribs to encourage the dog to breathe through their mouth to help shorten an episode.

04) *Hypothyroidism: is a condition resulting from an inadequate production of thyroid hormone, which is treated with medication. Symptoms can include weight gain or obesity, constant hunger, reduced energy and a coarser the feel of the dog's coat texture. Blood samples will be taken in order to test for a malfunctioning thyroid.

05) *Cherry Eye: many breeds can suffer from this genetic eye problem, including the Bulldog, where the gland of the third eyelid prolapses or slips in the corner of the eye, as a result of weakness of the connective tissue surrounding the gland, causing a pink fleshy protrusion to extend or bulge over the edge of the dog's eyelid.

Although it is possible for this problem to self-correct, it is recommended to take your dog to the veterinarian as soon as you notice this condition because treatment will require pushing the prolapsed gland back into the pocket.

06) *Entropion: is a condition in which the dog's eyelid will roll inward which then causes the lashes to rub against the eyeball. Left untreated, this condition can severely damage the dog's eye, even causing blindness. Surgery is required to correct this problem.

07) *Ectropion: in a dog suffering from this condition the lower eyelid will turn outward and requires surgery to repair.SEP SEP

08) Proptosis: is a problem occurring in short nosed breeds, such as the English Bulldog, when the dog's eyeball literally pops out of the eye socket trapping the eyelids behind the eyeball. SEP SEP

This is a condition that usually occurs as a result of injury or trauma to the dog's head. While chances of retaining eyesight are poor, if immediate veterinary attention is sought there is a slight chance that eyesight will remain.

09) *Cataracts: usually appear between the ages of two and four years and are common in many breeds. This is an eye condition where the lens becomes cloudy or milky, which would be like trying to see through a foggy window. This eye condition can appear from birth to 3 years of age and will usually lead to blindness.

10) Persistent Pupillary Membranes: this inherited disease is caused when remnants of fetal membrane (a source of blood supply for the fetus) continue to persist after birth of the puppy. Under normal circumstances this membrane atrophies between birth and 4 to 8 weeks, but when the atrophy is not complete, strands of the membrane connect to the lens of the eye, which can then cause cataracts.

11) Breathing Problems: due to their short muzzles, have compact breathing passageways, which leaves this breed prone to many breathing difficulties, including the inability to effectively regulate their temperature during hot weather by panting. This dog should not be exercised during hot weather unless there is shade and plenty of water available.

Further, because Bulldog breathing problems can be greatly worsened by the stresses of airplane travel in a cargo hold, that can lead to death, some airlines will no longer permit Pugs to travel inside the cargo hold if conditions are likely to cause heightened temperatures.

12) Pinched Nostrils (Stenotic Nares): some English Bulldogs will be born with pinched nostrils, and this condition can cause difficult or labored breathing. In more serious cases, a dog could faint or pass out from not receiving an adequate amount of air and in these cases surgery may be required to modify the obstructed breathing passages.

13) Skin Fold Dermatitis: Bulldogs are susceptible to bacterial and fungal infections. Many times, these infections occur in areas underneath their heavy skin folds on the muzzle and head, tail area or other areas of heavy wrinkles. It is also common on the paws and tail. These areas must be cleaned daily and kept dry to prevent infections, and a Bulldog should only be bathed when necessary.

14) Hemivertebrae: Bulldogs and other breeds with corkscrew tails, such as the Pug are an example of a hemivertebrae. If this condition occurs in a different area of the dog's spine, as a result of two pieces of the spinal vertebra not fusing together in a growing puppy, a cavity is formed in the spine, which then could place pressure on the dog's spinal cord, with the outcome usually causing paralysis.

15) *Bloat: is a life-threatening, common occurrence that can affect any deep-chested canine, such as the Bulldog, and 50% of dogs that develop bloat do not survive. This condition can happen very quickly, especially if you feed your dog right after vigorous exercise, or if they are a very fast eater and gulp in large quantities of air with their food.

Bloat is a serious, life-threatening condition that requires immediate veterinary intervention. If you have a deep chested dog that tends to gulp their food, get them a slow feeder type of bowl to slow down their eating process and never feed them immediately after exercise or having had a large drink of water.

16) *Obesity: many dogs are overweight, simply because they love to eat and when love of eating is combined with little or no exercise, which then leads to laziness, much like us humans, they will easily become obese. While obesity is a serious condition that plagues many breeds of dogs, the Bulldog seems to be more prone to this health problem.

17) Heart Disease and Cancer: according to statistics, 20% of Bulldogs succumb to heart related illnesses, with cancer causing death in another 18% of the breed.

18) Dental Problems: the English Bulldog can suffer from abnormal number, placement and development of teeth, which can require removal of teeth.

19) Dystocia: the female English Bulldog most often suffers from complications during the birth process, in which a high percentage of births (80-95%) must be performed through C-section.

20) Hydrocephalus: is a condition affecting the brain as a result of abnormal amounts of accumulated fluid causing pressure on the brain. Often it is difficult to diagnose, especially if the symptoms are mild and as a result the outcome of a dog suffering from hydrocephalus can vary considerably.

For instance, if the cause is due to injury or an infection that can be treated, the prognosis for recovery can be quite good, whereas if the cause is congenital and it is accompanied with obvious symptoms that have caused severe brain damage, the outlook will understandably be very poor.

21) Pyloric Stenosis: is a genetic condition where the opening leading from the stomach is narrowed or blocked and cannot function properly. More males suffer from this health condition than females.

A dog suffering from this condition will vomit undigested food within a few hours of eating their food and treatment will require surgery, followed by careful management of the dog's food intake.

3. Allergies
One of the most common complaints discussed at the veterinarian's office when they see dogs scratching and chewing at themselves is possible allergies.

Unlike us humans, who react to allergies with nasal symptoms, when our dogs are suffering from allergies they will typically present with itchy skin or ear problems.

a) Environmental: Allergies are usually first noticed because your dog is scratching, itching, biting, licking or chewing at their skin or paws.

Just like us humans, our dogs can develop allergies to dust, chemicals, grass, mold, pollen, car exhaust, cigarette smoke, and flea and tick preparations, as well as allergies to materials, such as wool or cotton, and chemicals found in washing soap or chemicals found in cleaning products you use around your home.

Symptoms are usually seen on the stomach, inside of the legs, and at the tail or paws.

Since most allergies are seasonal, our dogs will be more affected in the spring or fall. Airborne irritants inhaled by your Beabull, may result in coughing, sneezing or watery eyes.

If you think that your dog may have come in contact with an environmental irritant, the best thing you can do for your dog is give them a cleansing bath, with the proper canine shampoo, followed by canine conditioner.

Remember that dogs are closer to the ground, and the longer their hair, the more they resemble a duster who attracts everything they come into contact with.

b) Junk Food: *"True"* food allergies usually account for only about 10% of allergy problems in our canine friends.

For instance, itching, chewing and chronic ear infections are not actually caused by food allergies, but rather are the result of a suppressed immune system, which is caused by eating a low quality diet. These types of food allergies can oftentimes be completely resolved by changing your dog's diet to a high quality food that is more easily digested.

Proper nutrition is the easiest way to prevent any food allergies. Many dog food products contain corn, wheat and soybeans, which are common allergens. Usually it is the gluten in these foods that cause the allergic reaction.

Visit your local pet food store and educate yourself or talk with a knowledgeable representative because there's no excuse for feeding your dog a junk food diet when there are so many healthy choices now available that will help your canine companion live a long and healthy life.

4. Canine CPR

Of course, nobody wants to ever be put in a situation where the life of their precious canine companion is put at risk, however, the reality is that accidents happen, and therefore, knowing a little bit about how to help save your beloved furry friend is time well spent.

First of all, remember to handle an injured dog very carefully and gently. A dog that is traumatized, fearful or in pain, even one that is usually gentle, may lash out and try to bite.

Consider taking a class, because there are many animal CPR courses being offered these days through community educational systems or even online.

It's also a good idea to have a canine first aid kit both at home and in your vehicle in case of emergencies. Items to include in your first aid kit:

- Scissors
- Tweezers
- Tick Twister
- Nail Clippers
- Kwik Stop Styptic powder
- Gauze bandaging
- Non-stick bandages for wounds
- Medical tape
- Antiseptic wash for wounds, such as hydrogen peroxide
- Sterile eyewash
- Towel
- Washcloth
- Blanket

Familiarizing yourself with the American Red Cross emergency techniques outlined in the following chart *("Saving your pet with CPR")* may be exactly what you need to help save the life of your own dog or someone else's.

Saving your pet with CPR

With pets increasingly being treated like a member of the family, many owners are learning emergency techniques like CPR to keep their pet alive before bringing it to a veterinarian.

If there is no breathing and no pulse, begin CPR immediately.

Areas to check for pulse

Pupils

Gums

Check for breathing and pulse

Check pulse using middle and index finger below the wrist, inner thigh (femoral artery), below the ankle or where left elbow touches the chest.

Look for other warning signs

· Gums and lips will appear gray- colored.
· Pupils will be dilated and not responsive to light.

If not breathing, give breath to animal

Cats and small dogs
Place your mouth over its nose and mouth to blow air in.

Medium–large dogs
Place your mouth over its nose to blow air in.

Heimlich maneuver

If breath won't go in, airway may be blocked. Turn dog upside down, with its back against your chest. Wrap your arms around the dog and clasp your hands together just below its rib cage (since you're holding the dog upside down, it's above the rib cage, in the abdomen). Using both arms, give five sharp thrusts to the abdomen. Then check its mouth or airway for the object. If you see it, remove it and give two more rescue breaths.

Start compressions if no pulse

Lay animal on right side and place hand over ribs where its elbow touches the chest. Begin compressions. Do not give compressions if dog has pulse.

Animal size	Compress chest	Compressions per breath of air
Cat/small dog (Under 30 lbs.)	1/2-1 inch	5
Medium–large dog (30–90 lbs.)	1–3 inches	5
Giant dog (over 90 lbs.)	1–3 inches	10

Repeat procedure
· Check pulse after 1 minute and then every few minutes.
· Continue giving CPR until the animal has a pulse and is breathing.
· Stop CPR after 20 minutes.

SOURCE: American Red Cross

Chapter 9: Daily Feeding and Care

1. Feeding Puppies

For growing puppies, a general feeding rule of thumb is to feed 10% of the puppy's present body weight or between 2% and 3% of their projected adult weight each day.

Keep in mind that high energy puppies will require extra protein to help them grow and develop into healthy adult dogs, especially during their first two years of life.

There are now many foods on the market that are formulated for all stages of a dog's life (including the puppy stage), so whether you choose one of these foods or a food specially formulated for puppies, they will need to be fed smaller meals more frequently throughout the day (3 or 4 times), until they are at least one year of age.

NOTE: choose quality sources of meat protein for healthy puppies and dogs, including beef, buffalo, chicken, duck, fish, hare, lamb, ostrich, pork, rabbit, turkey, venison, or any other source of wild meaty protein.

2. Feeding Adults

An adult dog will generally need to be fed between 2% and 3% of their body weight each day. Read the labels and avoid foods that contain a high amount of grains and other fillers. Choose foods that list high quality meat protein as the main ingredient.

Picky Eaters: be careful that you do not get into the habit of *"doctoring"* your dog's food, which means adding bits and pieces of your human food to make it more tempting for your dog, otherwise, you will inadvertently create a picky eater who will then refuse to eat.

If this has already happened and your dog is refusing to eat his or her dog dinner, so long as you are feeding a high quality (mostly meat) dog food, do not worry, because no dog will starve itself. In fact, if the dog was living in the wild, they often will go 2-3 days without catching any food.

In order to break a dog of the habit of being a picky eater, make sure that you set regular meal times and remove food not eaten approximately 20 minutes after you have presented it to your dog.

It's important that your dog understands that you are in control of their food source, and once they understand this, they will also understand that they have a certain amount of time in which to eat their food.

With this "foodie" you will want to make certain that you never leave food unattended, and that you do not overfeed and under-exercise, because if you do, you will soon have an overweight dog.

It is also important to mix your dog's food with your hands, so that your scent is all over the food, before you give it to them to eat. This way you are mimicking what would happen if you were the pack leader out hunting for your food in the wild.

When dogs hunt for their own food, the leader of the pack always gets to eat first while all the other dogs must wait until the leader eats their fill before they can rush in to eat what is left over.

Therefore, when you are mixing your domesticated dog's dinner with your hands, and getting your scent all over the food, you are sending them the subtle message that you are the pack leader and that you are now allowing them to finish the food that was once yours.

TIP: grated Parmesan cheese sprinkled on a dog's dinner will help to stop picky eaters from ignoring their food while improving their skin and coat. To get the cheese to stick to the kibble, first mix a small amount of olive oil into the kibble, and then sprinkle with finely grated Parmesan cheese.

3. Treats

Since the creation of the first dog treat over 150 years ago the myriad of choices available on every pet store, feed store and grocery store shelf almost outnumbers those looking forward to eating them.

Today's treats are not just for making us guilty humans feel better because it makes us happy to give our fur friends something they really enjoy because today's treats are also designed to actually improve our dog's health.

Some of us humans treat our dogs, just because, others use treats for training purposes, others for health, while still others treat for a combination of reasons.

Whatever reason you choose to give treats to your Beabull, keep in mind that if we treat our dogs too often throughout the day, we may create a picky eater who will no longer want to eat their regular meals.

As well, if the treats we are giving are high calorie, we may be putting our dog's health in jeopardy by allowing them to become overweight.

TIP: an interesting article written by Jonathan O'Callaghan, recently published on June 12, 2014 in the Daily Mail, indicates that researchers in Sweden have discovered that dogs were visibly happier when they had to earn their treats as a reward for completing a task, rather than just being given a treat for looking cute.

Apparently, just like us humans get that happy "eureka" moment when we finally solve a problem, so do our canine counterparts.

If you've been treating your dog for no other reason that just because they looked expectantly at the cookie jar, perhaps now is the time to change your human habits and ask your dog to perform a trick or have to search for a hidden treat, so that your dog can also feel that emotional excitement of being rewarded for accomplishing a task.

4. Treats to Avoid

a) Rawhide: is soaked in an ash/lye solution to remove every particle of meat, fat and hair and then further soaked in bleach to remove remaining traces of the ash/lye solution. Now that the product is no longer food, it no longer has to comply with food regulations.

While the hide is still wet it is shaped into rawhide chews, and upon drying it shrinks to approximately 1/4 of its original size. Further, arsenic based products are often used as preservatives, and antibiotics and insecticides are added to kill bacteria that also fight against good bacteria in your dog's intestines.

The collagen fibers in the rawhide make it very tough and long lasting which makes this chew a popular choice for humans to give to their dogs because it satisfies the dog's natural urge to chew while providing many hours of quiet entertainment.

Sadly, when a dog chews a rawhide treat, they ingest many harsh chemicals and when your dog swallows a piece of rawhide, that piece now can swell up to four times its size inside your dog's stomach, which can cause anything from mild to severe gastric blockages that could become life threatening and require surgery.

b) Pig Ears: are actually the ears of pigs, and while most dogs will eagerly devour them, they are extremely high in fat, which can cause stomach upsets, vomiting and diarrhea for many dogs.

Pig ears are often processed and preserved with unhealthy chemicals that discerning dog guardians will not want to feed their dogs. As well, the ears are often quite thin and crispy and when the dog chews them pieces can break off, like chips, and can easily become stuck in a dog's throat.

While pig ears are generally not considered to be a healthy treat choice for any dog, they should be especially avoided for any dog that may be at risk of being overweight.

c) Hoof Treats: many humans give cow, horse and pig hooves to their dogs as treats because they consider them to be *"natural"* when the truth is that after processing these *"treats"* they retain little, if any, of their *"natural"* qualities.

Hoof treats are processed with harsh preservatives, including insecticides, lead, bleach, arsenic based products, and antibiotics to kill bacteria, that can also harm the good bacteria in your dog's intestines, and if all bacteria is not killed in these meat based products before feeding them to your dog, they could also suffer from Salmonella poisoning.

Hooves can also cause chipping or breaking of your dog's teeth as well as perforation or blockages in your dog's intestines.

5. Healthy Treats

Yes, we love to treat our dogs, whether for helping to teach the new puppy to go pee outside, teaching the adolescent dog new commands, for trick training, for general good behavior, or for no reason at all, other than that they just gave us the *"look"*.

a) Hard Treats: there are so many choices of hard, or crunchy treats available that come in many varieties of shapes, sizes and flavors, that you may have a difficult time choosing. If your dog will eat them, hard treats will help to keep their teeth cleaner.

Whatever you do choose, be certain to read the labels and make sure that the ingredients are high quality and appropriately sized for your Beabull friend.

b) Soft Treats: are also available in endless varieties and flavors, suitable for all the different needs of our fur friends and are often used for training purposes as they have a stronger smell.

c) Dental Treats or Chews: are designed with the specific purpose of helping your dog to maintain healthy teeth and gums. They usually require intensive chewing and are often shaped with high ridges and bumps to exercise the jaw and massage gums while removing plaque build-up near the gum line.

d) Freeze-Dried and Jerky Treats: offer a tasty morsel most dogs find irresistible as they are usually made of simple, meaty ingredients, such as liver, poultry and seafood.

These treats are usually lightweight and easy to carry around, which means they can also be great as training treats.

e) Human Food Treats: you will want to be very careful when feeding human foods to dogs as treats, because many of our foods contain additives and ingredients that could be toxic and harmful.

Be certain to choose simple, fresh foods with minimal or no processing, such as lean meat, poultry or seafood, and even if your dog will eat anything put in front of them, be aware that many common human foods, such as grapes, raisins, onions and chocolate are poisonous to dogs.

f) Training Treats: while any sort of treat can be used as an extra incentive during training sessions, soft treats are often used for training purposes because of their stronger smell and smaller sizes.

Generally, the treats you feed your dog should not make up more than approximately 10% of their daily food intake, so make sure the treats you choose are high quality, so that you can help to keep your Beabull both happy and healthy.

6. Choosing the Right Food
In order to choose the right food for your Beabull, first, it's important to understand a little bit about canine physiology and what Mother Nature intended when she created our fur friends.

More than 230 years ago, in 1785, the English Sportman's dictionary described the best diet for a dog's health in an article entitled *"Dog"*. This article indicated that the best food for a dog was something called *"Greaves"*, described as "the sediment of melted tallow. It is made into cakes for dogs' food. In Scotland and parts of the US it is called cracklings."

Out of the meager beginning of the first commercially made dog food has sprung a massively lucrative and vastly confusing industry that has only recently begun to evolve beyond those early days of feeding our dogs the dregs of human leftovers because it was cheap and convenient for us humans.

Even today, the majority of dog food choices have far more to do with being convenient for humans to store and serve than it does with being a diet truly designed to be a nutritionally balanced, healthy food choice for a canine.

The dog food industry is big business and as such, because there are now almost limitless choices, there is much confusion and endless debate when it comes to answering the question, *"What is the best food for my dog?"* Educating yourself, by talking to experts and reading everything you can find on the subject, plus taking into consideration several relevant factors, will help to answer the dog food question for you and your dog.

For instance, where you live may dictate what sorts of foods you have access to. Other factors to consider will include the particular requirements of your dog, such as their age, energy and activity levels.

Next will be expense, time and quality. While we all want to give our dogs the best food possible, many humans lead very busy lives and cannot, for instance, prepare their own dog food, but still want to feed a high quality diet that fits within their budget.

However, perhaps most important when choosing an appropriate diet for our dogs, is learning to be more observant of Mother Nature's design and taking a closer look at our dog's teeth, jaws and digestive tract in order to truly understand what is best for our dog's.

While humans are herbivores who derive energy from eating plants, our canine companions are carnivores, which means that they derive their energy and nutrient requirements from eating a diet consisting mainly or exclusively of the flesh of animal tissues (in other words, meat).

a) The Canine Teeth: the first part of your dog you will want to take a good look at when considering what to feed will be their teeth.

Unlike humans, who are equipped with wide, flat molars for grinding grains, vegetables and other plant-based materials, canine teeth are all pointed because they are designed to rip, shred and tear into animal meat and bone.

b) The Canine Jaw: is another obvious consideration when choosing an appropriate food source for our fur friends, is the fact that every canine is born equipped with powerful jaws and neck muscles for the specific purpose of being able to pull down and tear apart their hunted prey.

The structure of the jaw of every canine is such that it opens widely to hold large pieces of meat and bone, while the actual mechanics of a dog's jaw permits only vertical (up and down) movement that is designed for crushing.

c) The Canine Digestive Tract: a dog's digestive tract is short and simple and designed to move their natural choice of food (hide, meat and bone) quickly through their systems.

Vegetables and plant matter require more time to break down in the gastrointestinal tract, which in turn, requires a more complex digestive system than the canine body is equipped with.

The canine digestive system is simply unable to break down vegetable matter, which is why whole vegetables look pretty much the same going into your dog as they do coming out the other end.

Given the choice, most dogs would never choose to eat plants or vegetables and fruits over meat, however, we humans continue to feed them a kibble based diet that contains high amounts of vegetables, fruits and grains and low amounts of meat.

Plus, in order to get our dogs to eat fruits, vegetables and grains we usually have to flavor the food with meat or meat by-products.

How much healthier and long lived might our beloved fur friends be if, instead of largely ignoring nature's design for our canine companions, we chose to feed them whole, unprocessed, species-appropriate food?

With many hundreds of dog food brands to choose from, it's no wonder we humans are confused about what to feed our dogs to help them live long and healthy lives.

Following are some suggestions and questions that may help you choose a dog food company that you can feel comfortable with:

- How long have they have been in business?
- Is dog food their main industry?
- Are they dedicated to their brand?
- Are they easily accessible?
- Do they honestly answer your questions?
- Do they have a good Company Safety Standard?
- Do they set higher standards?
- Read the ingredients - where did they come from?
- Are the ingredients something you would eat?
- Are the ingredients farmed locally?
- Was it cooked using standards you would trust?
- Is the company certified under human food or organic guidelines?

Whatever you decide to feed your Beabull, keep in mind that, just as too much wheat, other grains and other fillers in our human diet is having detrimental effects on our human health, the same can be very true for our best fur friends.

Our dogs are also suffering from many of the same life threatening diseases that are commonly found in our human society (heart disease, cancer, diabetes, obesity), which all have a direct correlation to eating genetically altered foods that are no longer pure, in favor of a convenient, processed and packaged diet.

7. The Raw Diet

While more and more of us humans are coming to the belief that we are killing ourselves and our dogs with processed foods, others believe that there are dangers involved in feeding raw foods to our fur friends.

Those who are raw feeding advocates believe that the ideal diet for their dog is one which would be very similar to what a dog living in the wild would have access to hunting or foraging, and these canine guardians are often opposed to feeding their dog any sort of commercially manufactured pet foods, because they consider them to be poor substitutes.

On the other hand, those opposed to feeding their dogs a raw or biologically appropriate raw food diet, believe that the risks associated with food-borne illnesses during the handling and feeding of raw meats outweigh the purported benefits.

Interestingly, even though the United States Food and Drug Administration (FDA) states that they do not advocate a raw diet for dogs, they do advise for those who wish to take this route, that following basic hygiene guidelines for handling raw meat can minimize any associated risks.

Further, high pressure pasteurization (HPP), which is high pressure, water based technology for killing bacteria, is USDA-approved for use on organic and natural food products, and is being utilized by many commercial raw pet food manufacturers.

Interestingly, raw meats purchased at your local grocery store contain a much higher level of acceptable bacteria than raw food produced for dogs because the meat purchased for human consumption is supposed to be cooked, which will kill any bacteria that might be present.

This means that canine guardians feeding their dogs a raw food diet can be quite certain that commercially prepared raw foods sold in pet stores will be safer than raw meats purchased in grocery stores.

Many guardians of high energy, working breed dogs will agree that their dogs thrive on a raw or BARF (Biologically Appropriate Raw Food) diet and strongly believe that the potential benefits of feeding a raw dog food diet are many, including:

- Healthy, shiny coats
- Decreased shedding
- Fewer allergy problems
- Healthier skin
- Cleaner teeth
- Fresher breath
- Increased energy levels
- Improved digestion
- Smaller stools
- Strengthened immune system
- Increased mobility in arthritic pets
- Increase or improvement in overall health

All dogs, of every size, whether working breed or companion dogs are amazing athletes in their own right, therefore every dog deserves to be fed the best food available.

A raw diet is a direct evolution of what dogs ate before they became our domesticated pets and we turned toward commercially prepared, easy to serve dry dog food that required no special storage or preparation.

The BARF diet is all about feeding our dogs what they are designed to eat by returning them to their wild, evolutionary diet.

8. The Dehydrated Diet

Dehydrated dog food comes in both raw meat and cooked meat forms and these foods are usually air dried to reduce moisture to the level where bacterial growth is inhibited.

The appearance of de-hydrated dog food is very similar to dry kibble and the typical feeding methods include adding warm water before serving, which makes this type of diet both healthy for our dogs and convenient for us to serve.

Dehydrated recipes are made from minimally processed fresh whole foods to create a healthy and nutritionally balanced meal that will meet or exceed the dietary requirements of a healthy canine.

Dehydrating removes only the moisture from the fresh ingredients, which usually means that because the food has not already been cooked at a high temperature, more of the overall nutrition is retained.

A dehydrated diet is a convenient way to feed your dog a nutritious diet because all you have to do is add warm water, and wait five minutes while the food re-hydrates so your Beabull can enjoy a warm meal.

9. The Kibble Diet

While many canine guardians are starting to take a closer look at the food choices they are making for their furry companions, there is no mistaking that the convenience and relative economy of dry dog food kibble, that had its beginnings in the 1940's, continues to be the most popular pet food choice for most dog friendly humans.

Some 75 years later, the massive pet food industry offers up a confusingly large number of choices with hundreds of different manufacturers and brand names lining the shelves of veterinarian offices, grocery stores and pet food aisles.

NOTE: as a general rule of thumb, the best pet foods are NOT found in the grocery isle of your local supermarket. Take the time to buy your food from a trusted pet store and be sure to carefully read the labels so that you are not feeding your beloved fur friend an inferior food that could be harmful to their health.

While feeding a high quality bagged kibble diet that has been flavored to appeal to dogs and supplemented with vegetables and fruits to appeal to humans, may keep most Beabull companions happy and relatively healthy, you will ultimately need to decide whether this is the best diet for them.

10. The Right Bowl

Following is a brief description of the different categories and types of dog bowls that would be appropriate choices for your Beabull's particular needs.

Automatic Watering Bowls: are standard dog bowls (often made out of plastic) that are attached to a reservoir container, which is designed to keep water constantly available to your dog as long as there is water remaining in the storage compartment.

Ceramic/Stoneware Bowls: an excellent choice for those who like options in personality, color and shape.

Elevated Bowls: raised dining table dog bowls are a tidy and classy choice that will make your dog's dinner time a more comfortable experience while getting the bowls off the floor.

No Skid Bowls: are for dogs that push their bowls across the floor when eating. A non-skid dog bowl will help keep the feed bowl where you put it.

No Tip Bowls: are designed to prevent the messy type of doggy eater from flipping over their dinner or water bowls.

Slow Feeder Bowls: Many of our canine companions eat their food so quickly that it can literally cause health issues, such as choking, digestion problems, throwing up, and bloat that can cause death from gulping too much air with their food. This could definitely be a concern with the Beabull.

These specialty bowls are known by several different names, including *"Anti-Gulp"*, *"Go Slow"*, *"Slow Feeder"*, and *"Slow Me Down"*, and if your dog is wolfing their food, this will be the best type of feed bowl to slow down the dog that hoovers down their dinner in record time.

TIP: if you don't want to spend the money on a specialty slow feeder bowl, find yourself a fist-sized, smooth round rock and place it in the middle of your dog's stainless bowl so they have to work their way around the rock to get to their food. This will do the job of slowing them down just as effectively.

Stainless Steel Bowls: are as close to indestructible as a bowl can be, plus they are sanitary, easy to clean and water stays cooler for a longer period of time in a stainless bowl.

Wooden Bowls: for those humans concerned about stylish home decor, wooden dog bowl dining stations are beautiful pieces of furniture unto themselves that can enhance your home decor.

Travel Bowls: are convenient, practical and handy additions for every canine travel kit.

Consider a space saving, collapsible dog bowl, made out of hygienic, renewable bamboo that comes in fun colors and different sizes, making it perfect for every travel bowl needs.

If you would like to learn more about all the many dog bowl choices available, visit AskBoris.com, which is a comprehensive, one-stop website dedicated to everything dog, including food bowl choices, and helping you find just what you need for all your dog's requirements.

11. Exercise

All of our canine companions are amazing, natural athletes and because of this, they need daily exercise to stay fit, happy and healthy.

The highly energetic Beabull is no exception to this rule. Most every dog needs plenty of daily exercise, and will love going for walks or engaging in any manner of canine sport with their guardian several times every day.

As well, taking your Beabull for a disciplined walk, where they are on leash and calmly walking beside you without straining on the leash or trying to lead you, will reinforce that you are the boss and they are the follower.

Any type of disciplined exercise you can engage in with your dog will help to exercise both their body and their intelligent mind and will burn off pent up daily energy reserves so that your dog will be a happy and contented companion.

If you find that your dog is being a pest by chewing inappropriate items around the home or being demanding of your time, or especially unruly when visitors come to call, this is likely because they are not being challenged enough or exercised often enough, or long enough each day to drain out their daily pent up energy reserves.

A healthy, adult Beabull will thrive when being walked several times each day and will enjoy the challenge of being engaged in other forms of play and disciplined activity, such as fetch or search games, and they may even excel at the canine sport of Barn Hunt. Each dog will be different, therefore, in order to give him or her the best life, you will need to discover what sorts of activities they prefer and could excel at.

12. Playtime

Every dog needs some regular playtime each day, and this is even more important with a playful breed, such as the Beabull, who will be your loving, curious companion.

While every dog will be different with respect to what types of games they may enjoy, most will really love any game involving fetching or retrieving and it would be the rare Beabull that did not live for the opportunity to follow an interesting scent.

A fun game of *"Search"*, where you ask your dog to "Sit/Stay" while you hide a favorite treat that they then have to use their nose to find, will appeal to almost every dog.

After a disciplined walk with your dog, they will also enjoy being given the opportunity for some off leash freedom to really stretch out by running free to play and socialize with other similar sized dogs.

13. Daily Grooming

Daily grooming is a must for any healthy Beabull. Get into the routine of spending at least 10 minutes each day brushing your dog, and checking the teeth, ears and nails.

14. Safe Traveling

Far too many canine guardians do nothing to protect their companions when traveling with them inside their vehicles and now, some cities are fining vehicle operators for allowing their dogs to be free inside their vehicle when they are in motion because this is considered distracted driving.

According to a 2011 American Automobile Association study, only about 16% of dog owners restrain their pets when riding in a vehicle, and of those who are trying, many are not properly securing their beloved pets. That leaves 84% of people who let their dogs roam freely about the inside of their vehicles, leaving them at serious risk of being injured or killed in an automobile accident.

For example, when a vehicle traveling at only 30 miles per hour (48.28 kilometers per hour) is involved in an accident, a small, ten pound (4.54 kg), unrestrained dog will be subjected to approximately 300 pounds force (136 kilogram-force), which is certainly enough to seriously injure or kill a puppy or dog.

There is no denying that dogs that are not properly restrained become projectiles in any sort of vehicle crash.

As well, many drivers permit their smaller dogs to sit on their lap when driving, which is not only distracting to the driver, but if involved in an accident, the vehicle's airbags will deploy at 300 mph (482.8 kilometers per hour) which can easily snap the neck of a small dog.

a) Faulty Restraints: many dog lovers may be laboring under the misconception that they are doing the right thing by buckling their canine companions into a safety harness because they are unaware that many of these dog harnesses that are supposed to keep furry passengers safe have a 100% failure rate.

Statistics collected by the Center for Pet Safety (CPS) have shown that every popular restraint tested with dog dummies, traveling at a sedate 30 mph (48.28 km/h), not only failed, but also indicated that serious injuries or deaths were highly likely.

Most restraints that were tested in the CPS study allowed dogs to easily become flying projectiles during vehicle accidents because the harnesses were simply not strong enough to keep them in their seats, and in many cases the restraints could actually choke the dog during a crash.

When the MGA Research Corporation carried out a pilot study for The Center for Pet Safety (CPS), in which they tested 12 major brands of pet harnesses, the results indicated a **100% failure rate**.

According to the American Kennel Club, these safety harness tests were carried out using the average weights of the ten most popular breeds of dogs.

The founder and chairman of CPS, believes that, "Saying that these products prevent your pet from becoming a projectile in an accident is a potentially misleading statement."

Law enforcement agencies, safety advocates, insurance companies, and concerned dog owners need to keep pressing for the development of a standard for dog safety equipment, to insist that all such equipment pass a government regulated crash test before being sold as safe for travel.

The safest travel arrangement for any dog is to secure them inside a kennel, followed by finding a safety restraint that is crash and strength tested and certified to be safe for your dog.

b) Kennels: if you opt to contain your best friend inside a kennel, crate or travel bag, you absolutely must make sure that the kennel or bag is very securely attached with the vehicle's seatbelt system or even better, with special tie downs that are bolted to the floor of the vehicle.

A dog kennel or crate will easily fit (sideways) on the back seat of most vehicles and can be secured with the vehicle's restraint system, and a dog riding inside a kennel that is secure inside your vehicle will have the best protection in the case of a rollover accident, plus you will avoid the fines some locations are now charging for allowing a dog to roam freely inside a moving vehicle.

As well, for maximum safety and security when travelling with your dog, you might wish to go the extra mile and spend the extra dollars to buy them a "Mim VarioCage" (above).

The Mim VarioCage (from Mighty Mite Dog Gear) is apparently the only dog travel cage on the market today that has been tested in both frontal and rear collisions. It has also been in a drop test, which simulates a rollover with a car, and crash tests have been carried out by the Technical Research Institute of Sweden. This kennel is designed to fit into the cargo carrying area of a vehicle.

c) Harness Restraints: the Kurgo Tru-Fit Smart harness has been crash and strength tested and with its steel nesting buckles has a tensile strength tested to withstand a force of 2250 pounds (1020 kilogram-force). The crash test videos of this product depict a 35-pound (15.9 kilogram) dummy dog traveling at 30 miles per hour (48.28 km/h), recorded at an accredited University test facility.

The Ruff Rider Roadie® harness successfully passed the preliminary test criteria for both dynamic and static load limits. Ruff Rider's only product is the Roadie® travel restraint which was invented by dog owner, Carl Goldberg, after his pet was ejected through the front windshield of his vehicle during a minor collision.

The design of the Roadie® is so unique that it was awarded three (3) patents, and over the past 20 years Roadie® has helped protect many dogs during vehicle accidents.

Sleepypod™ manufactures a safety harness called *"Clickit Utility"* that has a #1 safety rating. Apparently, this harness is the first dog safety harness to incorporate three-points of attachment to better absorb force caused in a front end collision by effectively dissipating energy while keeping the dog in the car seat during an impact (patents pending).

The Clickit Utility harness can also be used in the cargo area and includes a d-ring on the back of the vest so it can be used as a walking harness.

Keep your dog safe when traveling in your vehicle. Do your research and either transport your dog inside a kennel, or find a safety harness that is both strength tested and certified to be able to keep your dog safe in the event of an accident.

d) Air Travel: while the Beabull will be too large to travel inside a Sherpa bag inside the airplane cabin, a smaller puppy could be *"carry on baggage"* if the carrier conforms to the airline regulations, which state that a pet carrier must be able to fit under the seat in front of you. Most soft carriers are airline approved and under seat dimensions are generally as follows:

Window Seat: 19" L x 14" W x 8.25" H
[48.26 cm L x 35.56 cm W x 20.955 cm H]
Middle Seat: 19" L x 19" W x 8.25" H
[48.26 cm L x 48.26 cm W x 20.955 cm H]
Aisle Seat: 19" L x 14" W x 8.25" H
[48.26 cm L x 35.56 cm W x 20.955 cm H]

For in-cabin travel by plane, your puppy must be able to stand up and turn around comfortably inside the bag. Airlines also require an absorbent liner in the bag, which could be a pee pad, an old towel, a favorite blanket, or a cozy, faux lambskin liner.

Many styles of canine carrier bags are officially approved for airline travel, and when you make your flight reservations, don't forget to reserve for your puppy as well because there is generally a small charge for in-cabin travel and some airlines will only permit a certain number of canine travelers per flight.

Dogs that are too large to fit inside a Sherpa bag will need to be transported inside a hard-sided kennel inside the airplane cargo hold.

Chapter 10: House Training

1. Human Training

House training, house breaking, or *"potty"* training, is a critical first step in the education of any new puppy, and the first part of a successful process is training the human guardian.

When you bring home your new Beabull puppy, they will be relying upon your guidance to teach them what they need to learn.

When you provide your puppy with your consistent patience and understanding, they are capable of learning rules at a very early age, and house training is no different, especially since it's all about establishing a regular routine.

Potty training a new puppy takes time and patience — how much time depends entirely upon you.

Check in with yourself and make sure your energy remains consistently calm and patient and that you exercise plenty of compassion and understanding while you help your new puppy learn their new bathroom rules.

Puppies and dogs flourish with routines and happily, so do humans, therefore, the first step will be to establish a daily routine that will work well for both canine and human alike.

For instance, depending upon the age of your puppy, make a plan to take them out for a bathroom break every two hours and stick to it because while you are in the beginning stages of potty training, the more vigilant and consistent you can be, the quicker and more successful your results will be.

Generally speaking, while your puppy is still growing, a young puppy can hold it approximately one hour for every month of their age.

This means that if your 2-month-old puppy has been happily snoozing for a couple of hours, as soon as they wake up, they will need to go outside. Some of the first indications or signs that your puppy needs to be taken outside to relieve themselves will be when you see them:
  • Sniffing around

- Circling
- Looking for or approaching the door
- Whining, crying or barking
- Acting agitated

It will be important to always take your puppy out first thing every morning, and immediately after they wake up from a nap as well as soon after they have finished eating a meal or having a big drink of water.

Also, your happy praise goes a long way toward encouraging and reinforcing future success when your puppy makes the right decisions, so let them know you are happy when they do their business in the right place.

Initially, treats can be a good way to reinforce how pleased you are that your puppy is learning to go potty in the right place. Slowly treats can be removed and replaced with your happy praise.

Next, now that you have a new puppy in your life, you will want to be flexible with respect to adapting your schedule to meet the requirements that will help to quickly teach your puppy their new bathroom routine.

This means not leaving your puppy alone for endless hours at a time because firstly, they are sensitive pack animals that need companionship and your direction at all times, plus long periods alone will result in the disruption of the potty training schedule you have worked hard to establish.

If you have no choice but to leave your puppy alone for many hours, make sure that you place them in a paper lined room or pen where they can relieve themselves without destroying your favorite carpet or new hardwood flooring.

Remember, your Beabull is a growing puppy with a bladder and bowels that they do not yet have complete control over and you will have a much happier time and better success if you simply train yourself to pay attention to when your young companion is showing signs of needing to relieve themselves.

2. Bell Training

A very easy way to introduce your new puppy to house training is to begin by teaching them how to ring a doorbell whenever they need to go outside.

Ringing a doorbell is not only a convenient alert system for both you and your puppy or dog, your visitors will be most impressed by how smart your dog is. A further benefit of training your puppy to ring a bell is that you will not have to listen to your puppy or dog whining, barking or howling to be let out, and your door will not become scratched up from their nails.

Unless you prefer to purchase an already manufactured doggy doorbell or system, take a trip to your local novelty store and purchase a small bell that has a nice, loud ring.

Attach the bell to a piece of ribbon or string and hang it from a door handle or tape it to a door sill near the door where you will be taking your puppy out when they need to relieve themselves. The string will need to be long enough so that your puppy can easily reach the bell with their nose or a paw.

Next, each time you take your puppy out to go potty, say the word *"Out"*, and use their paw or their nose to ring the bell. Praise them for this *"trick"* and immediately take them outside.

The only down side to teaching a puppy or dog to ring a bell when they want to go outside, is that even if they don't actually have to go out to relieve themselves, but just want to go outside because they are bored, you will still have to take them out every time they ring the bell.

There are many types and styles of *"gotta' go"* commercially manufactured bells you could choose, ranging from the elegant **"Poochie Bells™"** that hang from a doorknob, the simple **"Tell Bell™"** that sits on the floor, or various high tech door chime systems that function much like a doggy intercom system where they push a pad with their paw and it rings a bell.

Whatever doorbell system you choose for your puppy, once they are trained, this type of an alert system is an easy way to eliminate accidents in the home.

3. Kennel Training

Kennel training is always a good idea for any puppy early in their education, because it can be utilized for many different situations, including keeping them safe while traveling inside a vehicle and being a very helpful tool for house training.

When purchasing a kennel for your puppy, always buy a kennel that will be the correct size for your puppy once they become an adult. The kennel will be the correct size if an adult Beabull can stand up and easily turn around inside their kennel.

When you train your puppy to accept sleeping in their own kennel at nighttime, this will also help to accelerate their potty training, because no puppy or dog wants to relieve themselves where they sleep, which means that they will hold their bladder and bowels as long as they possibly can.

Always be kind and compassionate and remember that a puppy will be able to hold it approximately one hour for every month of their age. Generally, a puppy that is three months old will be able to hold it for approximately three hours, unless they just ate a meal or had a big drink of water.

Be watchful and consistent so that you learn your puppy's body language, which will alert you to when it's time for them to go outside.

Presenting them with familiar scents, by taking them to the same spot in the yard or the same street corner, will help to remind and encourage them that they are outside to relieve themselves.

Use a voice cue to remind your puppy why they are outside, such as *"go pee"* and always remember to praise them every time they relieve themselves in the right place so that they quickly understand what you expect of them and will learn to *"go"* on cue.

4. Exercise Pen Training

The exercise pen is a transition from kennel only training and will be helpful for those times when you may have to leave your puppy for more hours than they can reasonably be expected to hold it.

During those times when you must be away from the home for several hours, it's time to introduce your puppy to an exercise pen.

Exercise pens are usually constructed of wire sections that you can put together in whatever shape you desire, and the pen needs to be large enough to hold your puppy's kennel inside one half of the pen, while the other half will be lined with newspapers or pee pads.

Place your puppy's food and water dishes next to the kennel and leave the kennel door open, so they can wander in and out whenever they wish, to eat or drink or go to the papers or pads if they need to relieve themselves.

Your puppy will be contained in a small area of your home while you are away and because they are already used to sleeping inside their kennel, they will not want to relieve themselves inside the area where they sleep. Therefore, your puppy will naturally go to the other half of the pen to relieve themselves on the newspapers or pee pads.

This method will help train your puppy to be quickly "paper" trained when you must leave them alone for a few hours.

5. Puppy Apartment™ Training

A similar and more costly alternative, the *Puppy Apartment™* is a step up from the exercise pen training system that makes the process of crate or pen training even easier on both humans and puppies.

The Puppy Apartment™ works well in a variety of situations, whether you're at home and unable to pay close attention to your puppy's needs, whether you must be away from the home for a few hours or during the evening when everyone is asleep and you don't particularly want to get up at 3:00 a.m. to take your puppy out to go pee.

The Puppy Apartment™ is an innovation that is convenient for both puppy and human alike. What makes this system so effective is the patent pending dividing wall with a door leading to the other side, all inside the pen.

One side of the Puppy Apartment™ is where the puppy's bed is located and the other side (through the doorway) is the bathroom area that is lined with pee pads.

With the bathroom right next door, your puppy or dog can take a bathroom break whenever they wish, without the need to alert family members to let them out.

This one bedroom, one bathroom system, which is a combination of the kennel/training pen, is a great alternative for helping to eliminate the stress of worrying about always keeping a watchful eye on your puppy or getting up during the night to take them outside every few hours to help them avoid making mistakes.

According to Modern Puppies...

> *"The Puppy Apartment™ takes the MESSY out of paper training, the ODORS AND HASSLES out of artificial grass training, MISSING THE MARK out of potty pad training and HAVING TO HOLD IT out of crate training. House training a puppy has never been faster or easier!*

The Puppy Apartment™ has taken all the benefits of the most popular potty training methods and combined them into one magical device and potty training system. This device and system has revolutionized how modern puppies are potty trained!"

Manufactured in the United States, this product ships directly from the California supplier (Modern Puppies) and is only available online at Modern Puppies.

6. Free Training

If you would rather not confine your young puppy to one or two rooms in your home, and will be allowing them to freely range about your home anywhere they wish during the day, this is considered free training.

When free house training your puppy, you will need to closely watch your puppy's activities all day long so that you can be aware of the *"signs"* that will indicate when they need to go outside to relieve themselves. For instance, circling and sniffing is a sure sign that they are looking for a place to do their business.

Never get upset or scold a puppy for having an accident inside the home, because this will result in teaching your puppy to be afraid of you and to only relieve themselves in secret places or when you're not watching.

If you catch your puppy making a mistake, all that is necessary is for you to calmly say *"No"*, and quickly scoop them up and take them outside or to their indoor bathroom area.

From your sensitive puppy's point of view, yelling or screaming when they make a potty mistake, will be understood by your puppy or dog as unstable energy being displayed by the person who is supposed to be their leader. This type of unstable behavior will only teach your puppy to fear and disrespect you.

When you are vigilant, the Beabull should not be a difficult puppy to housebreak and they will generally do very well when you start them off with *"puppy pee pads"* that you will move closer and closer to the same door that you always use when taking them outside. This way they will quickly learn to associate going to this door when they need to relieve themselves.

When you train yourself to pay close attention to your puppy's sleeping, eating, drinking and playing habits, you will quickly learn their body language so that you are able to predict when they might need to relieve themselves.

Your puppy will always need to relieve themselves first thing in the morning, as soon as they wake up from a nap, approximately 20 minutes after they finish eating a meal, after they have finished a play session, and of course, before they go to bed at night.

It's important to have compassion during this house training time in your young dog's life so that their education will be as stress-free as possible. It's also important to be vigilant because how well you pay attention will minimize the opportunities your puppy may have for making a bathroom mistake in the first place, and the fewer mistakes they make, the sooner your puppy will be house trained.

7. Mistakes Happen

Remember that a dog's sense of smell is at least 2,000 times more sensitive that our human sense of smell. As a result of your puppy's superior sense of smell, it will be very important to effectively remove all odors from house training accidents, because otherwise, your puppy will be attracted by the smell to the place where they may have had a previous accident, and will want to do their business there again and again.

While there are many products that are supposed to remove odors and stains, many of these are not very effective. You want a professional grade cleaner that will not just mask one odor with another scent, you want a product that will completely neutralize odors.

TIP: go to RemoveUrineOdors.com and order yourself some *"SUN"* and/or *"Max Enzyme"* because these products contain professional-strength odor neutralizers and urine digesters that bind to and completely absorb odors on any type of surface.

8. Electronic Training Devices

Generally speaking, positive training methods are far more effective than using devices that involve negative stimulation.

Further, unless you are training a dog to field hunt in a large area where they cannot see you, using electronic devices is usually a excuse for a lazy human who will not take the time to properly train their dog by teaching them rules and boundaries which leads to respect and an attentive follower. When you do not provide your Beabull (or any dog) with a consistent leadership role that teaches your dog to trust, respect and listen to you in all circumstances, you will inevitably experience behavioral issues.

Electronic training devices such as e-collars, spray collars or electronic fencing all rely upon negative, painful or stressful reinforcement, which can easily cause any dog to become nervous or live a life of fear. For instance, a dog simply cannot understand the principles of "invisible" boundaries, and therefore, should never be subjected to the confusion of the punishment that occurs when walking across an invisible line within their own home territory.

Dogs naturally understand the positive training methods of receiving a reward, which is not only much more efficient and effective when teaching boundaries, rewards are far kinder, and create a much stronger bond with your dog.

a) The Truth About Shock Collars: first of all, it would have to be an extremely rare situation in which it would be necessary or recommended that you use a shock collar on a friendly Beabull as these devices are usually only employed in extreme situations, and generally for larger or more aggressive breeds who could seriously harm someone.

The use of remote, electronic, shock or *"e-collars"* is at best a controversial subject that can quickly escalate into heated arguments.

In certain, rare circumstances, and when used correctly, the e-collar can be a helpful training tool that could actually save a dog's life if they are acting out in dangerous ways that could seriously harm or even kill them.

An e-collar would generally be utilized in a circumstance where a larger breed of dog has access to free range over a large property, resulting in difficulties getting their attention from a distance if they become distracted by other animals or smells. Many dogs that have not been properly trained from a young age also learn that when they are off leash and out of your immediate reach that they can choose to ignore your commands, bark their heads off, terrorize the neighbors or chase wildlife.

While all of these situations may be activities that an untrained Beabull left to their own devices might be interested in pursuing, especially they have access to a large property and they catch an interesting scent on the wind, they would usually prefer being at home with their humans.
Generally e-collars can be effective training tools for working breed herding, hunting or tracking dogs and in these types of circumstances a

remote training collar can be an effective training device for reinforcing verbal commands from a great distance, such as "Come", "Sit" or "Stay".

Finally, electronic collars can be used as a last resort to help teach a dog not to engage in a dangerous behavior that could result in them being seriously harmed or even killed.

b) Electronic Fencing: honestly, there are far more reasons NOT to install an electronic fence as a means of keeping your dog inside your yard, than there are good reasons for considering one.

In most cases, humans who install electronic fencing because they are worried that their dog will run away have simply not taken the time to develop a relationship of trust and respect with their canine companion. For instance, a dog whose yard is surrounded by an electronic fence can quite easily develop fear, aggression, or both, directed toward what they may believe is the cause of the shock they are receiving. As a result, installing an electronic fence may cause your dog to become aggressive toward cats, other dogs, other humans, other wildlife, children riding by on bikes or skateboards, the mail carrier, or the people next door.

As well, a dog that receives a fright, or in excitement forgets about the shock they are going to receive, may run through an electronic fence and then be too frightened or stressed to come back home because it means that they must pass through the painful barrier again.

Further, it is actually possible that electronic fencing may encourage a dog to escape the yard simply because they associate their yard with pain. This feeling can be reinforced if a dog escapes the electronic yard and then is again punished by the shock when they attempt to come home.

Another factor to keep in mind with respect to electronic fencing is that other dogs or teasing children can freely enter the yard and torment or attack your dog, and a thief bent on stealing your friendly designer dog will be able to do so with ease.

The absolute best way to keep your dog safe in their own yard, while helping to establish your role as guardian and leader, is to be out there with them while they are on leash, and to only permit them freedom in your yard under your close supervision.

Chapter 11: Medical Care & Safety

1. Choosing a Veterinarian

A consideration to keep in mind when choosing a veterinarian clinic will be that some clinics specialize in caring for smaller pets, and some specialize in larger animal care, while still others have a wide ranging area of expertise and will care for all animals, including livestock and reptiles.

Choosing a clinic will be a personal decision, however, your dog's needs may be better served by choosing a clinic that specializes in the care of smaller domesticated pets.

Choosing a good veterinary clinic will be very similar to choosing the right health care clinic or doctor for your own personal health because you want to ensure that your puppy receives the quality care they deserve.

Begin your search by asking other dog owners where they take their fur friends and whether they are happy with the service they receive.

If you don't know anyone to ask, visit the local pet store in your area as they should be able to provide you with references and local listings of pet care clinics. Next, check online, because a good pet clinic will have an active website up and running that will list details of all the services they provide along with an overview of all staff members, their education and qualifications.

Once you've narrowed your search, it's time to personally visit the clinics you may be interested in, as this will be a good opportunity for you to visually inspect the facility, interact with the staff and perhaps meet the veterinarians face to face.

Of course, it's not just you who needs to feel comfortable with the clinic chosen and those working there. Your puppy needs to feel comfortable, too, and this is where visiting a clinic and interacting with the staff and veterinarians will provide you with an idea of their experience and expertise in handling your puppy.

If your puppy is comfortable with them, then you will be much more likely to trust that they will be providing the best care for your puppy who will need to receive all their vaccinations and yearly check-ups, and eventually be spayed or neutered.

It's also a good idea to take your puppy into your chosen clinic several times before they actually need to be there for any treatment, so that they are not fearful of the new smells and unfamiliar surroundings.

2. Neutering and Spaying

While it can sometimes be difficult to find the definitive answer when asking when is the best time to neuter or spay your young Beabull, because there are varying opinions on this topic, one thing that most veterinarians do agree on is that earlier spaying or neutering, between 4 and 6 months of age, is a better choice than waiting.

Spaying or neutering surgeries are carried out under general anesthesia, and as more dogs are being neutered at younger ages, speak with your veterinarian and ask for their recommendations regarding the right age to spay or neuter your dog, and following are some points to be aware of:

1) Effects on Aggression: intact (non-neutered and spayed) males and females are more likely to display aggression related to sexual behavior than are dogs that have been neutered or spayed.

Fighting, particularly in male dogs that is directed at other males, is less common after neutering, and the intensity of other types of aggression, such as irritable aggression in females will be totally eliminated by spaying.

While neutering or spaying is not a treatment for aggression, it can certainly help to minimize the severity and escalation of aggressiveness and is often the first step toward resolving an aggressive behavior problem.

2) What is Neutering? This surgical procedure, carried out by a licensed veterinarian surgeon, renders a male dog unable to reproduce.

In males, the surgery is also referred to as *"castration"* because the procedure entails the removal of the young dog's testicles. When the testicles are removed, what is left behind is an empty scrotal sac (which used to contain the puppy's testicles) and this empty sac will soon shrink in size until it is no longer noticeable.

3) Neutering Males: neutering a male puppy before they are six months of age can help to ensure that they will be less likely to suffer from obesity problems when they grow older. Neutering can also mean that a male dog will be less likely to have the urge to wander.

Further, waiting until a male dog is older than six months before having them neutered could mean that they will experience the effects of raging testosterone that will drive them to escape their yards by any means necessary to search out females to mate with.

Non-neutered males also tend to spray or mark territory much more often, both inside and outside the home, and during this time can start to display aggressive tendencies toward other dogs as well as people.

3) What is Spaying? In female puppies, sterilization, referred to as *"spaying,"* is a surgical procedure carried out by a licensed veterinarian, to prevent the female dog from becoming pregnant and to stop regular heat cycles.

The sterilization procedure is much more involved for a female puppy (than for a male), as it requires the removal of both ovaries and the uterus by incision into the puppy's abdominal cavity. The uterus is also removed during this surgery, to prevent the possibility of it becoming infected later on in life.

4) Spaying Females: preferably, a female puppy should be spayed before their very first estrus or heat cycle. Females in heat often appear more agitated and irritable, while sleeping and eating less and some may become extremely aggressive toward other dogs.

Spaying female puppies before their first heat pattern can eliminate these hormonal stressors and reduce the opportunity of mammary glandular tumors. Early spaying also protects against various other potential concerns, such as uterine infections.

5) Effects on General Temperament: many dog owners often become needlessly worried that a neutered or spayed dog will lose their vigor.

Rest assured that a dog's personality or energy level will not be modified or altered in any way by the neutering process, and in fact, many unfavorable qualities resulting from hormonal impact may resolve after surgery. Your Beabull will certainly not come to be less caring or cheerful, and neither will he or she resent you because you are not denying your dog any essential encounters. You will, however, be acting as a conscientious, informed, and caring guardian. Further, there is little evidence to suggest that the nature of a female Beabull will improve after having a litter of puppies.

What IS important is that you do not project your own psychological needs or concerns onto your puppy, because there is no gain to be had from permitting sexual activity in either male or female canines.

For instance, it is not *"abnormal"* or *"mean"* to manage a puppy's reproductive activity by having them sterilized. Rather, it is unkind and irresponsible not to neuter or spay a dog and there are many positive benefits of having this procedure carried out.

6) Effects on Escape and Roaming: a neutered or spayed dog is less likely to wander. Castrated male dogs have the tendency to patrol smaller sized outdoor areas and are less likely to participate in territorial conflicts with perceived opponents.

NOTE: a dog that has actually already experienced successful escapes from the yard may continue to wander after they are spayed or neutered.

7) Effects on Problem Elimination: an unsterilized dog may urinate or defecate inside the home or in other undesirable areas in an attempt to mark or stake territorial claims, relieve anxiety, or advertise their available reproductive status.

While neutering or spaying a puppy after they have already begun to inappropriately eliminate or mark territory to announce their sexual availability to other dogs will reduce the more powerful urine odor as well as eliminate the hormonal factors, once this habit has begun, the undesirable behavior may continue to persist after neutering or spaying.

8) Possible Weight Gain: while it is possible that metabolic changes that occur after spaying or neutering may cause some puppies to gain weight, often the real culprit for any weight gain is the human who feels guilty for subjecting their puppy to any kind of pain and therefore, they attempt to make themselves feel better by feeding more treats or meals to their canine companion.

If you are concerned about weight gain after neutering or spaying a Beabull puppy, simply adjust their food and treat consumption, as needed, and make sure that they receive adequate daily exercise.

It's a very simple process to change your dog's food intake according to their physical demands and how they look, and if your puppy's daily exercise and level of activity has not changed after they have been spayed or neutered, there will likely be no change in food management necessary.

9) Pediatric Spaying/Neutering: in the past, the usual time frame for neutering or spaying a puppy was between the ages of 5 and 6 months. However, even though there exists quite a bit of debate amongst veterinarians, pediatric spaying or neutering has become more widely accepted.

The American Veterinary Medical Association has supported this concept of very early sterilization since 2004 in an effort to help reduce the numbers of homeless, unwanted animals.

Pediatric spaying or neutering is also called *"prepuberal"* or "early" spaying or neutering and may be carried out at a much earlier age, usually between 6 and 14 weeks.

3. Why Vaccinate a Puppy?

Puppies need to be vaccinated by a veterinarian in order to provide them with protection against four common and serious diseases referred to as *"DAPP"*, which stands for **D**istemper, **A**denovirus, **P**arainfluenza and **P**arvo Virus.

Approximately one week after your puppy has completed all three sets of primary DAPP vaccinations they will be fully protected from those specific diseases. Thereafter, most veterinarians will recommend a once a year vaccination for the next year or two.

It has now become common practice to vaccinate adult dogs every three years, and if your veterinarian is insisting on a yearly vaccination for your puppy, you need to ask them why, because to do otherwise is considered by most professionals to be *"over vaccinating"*. Whether or not your dog actually needs a booster can be determined with a simple blood test.

4. Common Diseases and Viruses

a) Distemper: is a contagious and serious viral illness for which there is currently no known cure.

This deadly virus, which is spread either through the air or by direct or indirect contact with a dog that is already infected, or other distemper carrying wildlife, including ferrets, raccoons, foxes, skunks and wolves, is a relative of the measles virus which affects humans.

Canine distemper is sometimes also called *"hard pad disease"* because some strains of the distemper virus actually cause thickening of the pads on a dog's feet, which can also affect the end of a dog's nose.

In dogs or animals with weak immune systems, death may result two to five weeks after the initial distemper infection. Early symptoms of distemper include fever, loss of appetite, and mild eye inflammation that may only last a day or two. Symptoms become more serious and noticeable as the disease progresses.

A puppy or dog that survives the distemper virus will usually continue to experience symptoms or signs of the disease throughout their remaining lifespan, including *"hard pad disease"* as well as *"enamel hypoplasia"*, which is damage to the enamel of the puppy's teeth that are not yet formed or that have not yet pushed through the gums. Enamel hypoplasia is caused when the distemper virus kills the cells that manufacture tooth enamel.

b) Adenovirus: causes infectious canine hepatitis, which can range in severity from very mild to very serious, sometimes resulting in death.

Symptoms can include coughing, loss of appetite, increased thirst and urination, tiredness, runny eyes and nose, vomiting, bruising or bleeding under the skin, swelling of the head, neck and body, fluid accumulation in the abdomen area, jaundice (yellow tinge to the skin), a bluish clouding of the cornea of the eye (called "hepatitis blue eye") and seizures.

There is no specific treatment for infectious canine hepatitis. Treatment of the disease is focused on managing symptoms while the virus runs its course. Hospitalization and intravenous fluid therapy may be required in severe cases.

c) Canine Parainfluenza Virus (CPIV): also referred to as *"canine influenza virus"*, *"greyhound disease"* or *"race flu"*, which is easily spread through the air or by coming into contact with respiratory secretions, was originally a virus that only affected horses.

This disease is believed to have adapted to become contagious to dogs, is easily spread from dog to dog, and may cause symptoms that become fatal.

While the more frequent occurrences of this respiratory infection are seen in areas where there are high dog populations, such as race tracks, boarding kennels and pet stores, this virus is highly contagious to any dog or puppy, at any age.

Symptoms can include a dry, hacking cough, difficulty breathing, wheezing, runny nose and eyes, sneezing, fever, loss of appetite, tiredness, depression and possible pneumonia. In cases where only a cough exists, tests will be required to determine whether the cause of the cough is the parainfluenza virus or the less serious *"kennel cough"*.

While many dogs can naturally recover from this virus, they will remain contagious, and for this reason, in order to prevent the spread to other animals, aggressive treatment of the virus, with antibiotics and antiviral drugs will be the general course of action.

In more severe cases, a cough suppressant may be prescribed, as well as intravenous fluids to help prevent secondary bacterial infection.

d) Canine Parvovirus (CPV): is a highly contagious viral illness affecting puppies and dogs. Parvovirus also affects other canine species including foxes, coyotes and wolves. There are two forms of this virus (1) the more common intestinal form, and (2) the less common cardiac form, which can cause death in young puppies.

Symptoms of the intestinal form of parvovirus include vomiting, bloody diarrhea, weight loss, and lack of appetite, while the less common cardiac form attacks the heart muscle.

Early vaccination in young puppies has radically reduced the incidence of canine parvovirus infection, which is easily transmitted either by direct contact with an infected dog, or indirectly, by sniffing an infected dog's feces.

The virus can also be brought into a dog's environment on the bottom of human shoes that may have stepped on infected feces, and there is evidence that this hardy virus can live in ground soil for up to a year.

Recovery from parvovirus requires both aggressive and early treatment. With proper treatment, death rates are relatively low (between 5 and 20%), although chances of survival for puppies are much lower than for older dogs, and in all instances, there is no guarantee of survival.

Treatment of parvovirus requires hospitalization where intravenous fluids and nutrients are administered to help combat dehydration. As well, antibiotics will be given to counteract secondary bacterial infections, and as necessary, medications to control nausea and vomiting may also be given. Without prompt and proper treatment, dogs that have severe parvovirus infections can die within 48 to 72 hours.

5. Other Diseases and Viruses

a) Rabies: is a viral disease transmitted by coming into contact with the saliva of an infected animal, usually through a bite.

The virus travels to the brain along the nerves and once symptoms develop, death is almost certainly inevitable, usually following a prolonged period of suffering.

If you plan to travel out of State or across country borders, you will need to make sure that your dog has an up to date Rabies Vaccination Certificate (NASPHV form 51) indicating they have been inoculated against rabies.

Vaccinating dogs against rabies is also compulsory in most countries in mainland Europe, as is permanent identification and registration of dogs through the use of a Pet Passport. Those living in a country that is rabies free (UK, Eire) are not required to vaccinate their dogs against rabies, unless they intend to travel.

There is also a new study that has been carried out by Kansas State University veterinary diagnosticians, which finds that pets with out-of-date rabies vaccinations are *"very unlikely to develop the fatal disease if given a rabies booster immediately after exposure to the virus"*.

As a result of this new study, many dog lives may be saved. Now dogs that have been exposed to rabies, which would have previously been quarantined or euthanized because their rabies vaccination was not up to date, may instead be given a booster vaccination and monitored for 45 days at home.

b) Leishmaniasis: is caused by a parasite and is transmitted by a bite from a sand fly and there is no definitive answer for effectively combating Leishmaniasis, especially since one vaccine will not prevent the known multiple species. In areas where the known cause is a sand fly, deltamethrin collars (containing a neurotoxic insecticide) worn by the dogs has been proven to be 86% effective.

There are two types of Leishmaniasis: (1) a skin reaction causing hair loss, lesions and ulcerative dermatitis, and (2) a more severe, abdominal organ reaction, which is also known as *"black fever"*. When the disease affects organs of the abdominal cavity the symptoms include:

- Loss of appetite
- Diarrhea
- Severe weight loss
- Exercise intolerance
- Vomiting
- Nose bleed
- Tarry feces
- Fever
- Pain in the joints
- Excessive thirst and urination
- Inflammation of the muscles

Leishmaniasis spreads throughout the body to most organs, with kidney failure being the most common cause of death. Virtually all infected dogs develop this system wide disease and as much as 90% of those infected will also display skin reactions. Affected dogs in the US are frequently found to have acquired this infection in another country.

Of note, is that this disease is regularly found in the Middle East, the area around the Mediterranean basin, Portugal, Spain, Africa, South and Central America, southern Mexico and the US, with regular cases reported in Oklahoma and Ohio, where it is found in 20 to 40% of the dog population. There have also been a few reported cases in Switzerland, northern France and the Netherlands.

NOTE: Leishmaniasis is a *"zoonotic"* infection, which is a contagious disease that can be spread between both animals and humans. This means that the organisms residing in the Leishmaniasis lesions can be communicated to humans.

Treatment in dogs is often difficult and the dog may suffer from relapses. Leishmaniasis poses a significant risk to the health of your dog, especially if you travel to the Mediterranean.

c) Lyme Disease: is one of the most common tick-borne diseases in the world, which is transmitted by Borrelia bacteria found in the deer or sheep tick. Lyme disease, also called *"borreliosis"*, is also a zoonotic disease that can affect both humans and dogs and this disease can be fatal.

The Borrelia bacteria that causes Lyme's disease, is transmitted by slow-feeding, hard-shelled deer or sheep ticks, and the tick usually has to be attached to the dog for a minimum of 18 hours before the infection is transmitted.

Symptoms of this disease in a young or adult dog include:
- Recurrent lameness from joint inflammation
- Loss of appetite
- Depression
- Stiff walk with arched back
- Sensitivity to touch
- Swollen lymph nodes
- Fever
- Kidney damage
- Rare heart or nervous system complications

While Lyme disease has been reported in dogs throughout the United States and Europe, it is most prevalent in the upper Mid-Western states, the Atlantic seaboard, and the Pacific coastal states.

In order to properly diagnose and treat Lyme disease, blood tests will be required, and if the tests are positive, oral antibiotics will be prescribed to treat the conditions.

Prevention is the key to keeping this disease under control because dogs that have had Lyme disease before are still able to get the disease again. There is a vaccine for Lyme disease and dogs living in areas that have easy access to these ticks should be vaccinated yearly.

d) Rocky Mountain Spotted Fever (RMSF): is a tick-transmitted disease very often seen in dogs in the East, Midwest, and plains region of the US, and the organisms causing Rocky Mountain Spotted Fever (RMSF) are transmitted by both the American dog tick and the RMSF tick, which must be attached to the dog for a minimum of five hours in order to transmit the disease. Common symptoms of RMSF include:
- Fever
- Reduced appetite
- Depression
- Pain in the joints
- Lameness
- Vomiting
- Diarrhea

Some dogs affected with RMSF may develop heart abnormalities, pneumonia, kidney failure, liver damage, or even neurological signs, such as seizures or unsteady, wobbly or stumbling gait.

Diagnosis of this disease requires blood testing and if the results are positive, oral antibiotics will be given to the infected dog for approximately two weeks. Dogs that can clear the organism from their systems will recover and after being infected, will remain immune to future infection.

e) Ehrlichiosis: is a tick borne disease transmitted by both the brown dog tick and the Lone Star Tick.

Ehrlichiosis has been reported in every state in the US, as well as worldwide. Common symptoms include:
- Depression
- Reduced appetite
- Fever
- Stiff and painful joints
- Bruising

Signs of infection typically occur less than a month after a tick bite and last for approximately four weeks. There is no vaccine available.

Blood tests may be required to test for antibodies and treatment will require a course of antibiotics for up to four weeks in order to completely clear the organism from the infected dog's system.

After a dog has been previously infected, they may develop antibodies to the organism, but will not be immune to being re-infected.

Dogs living in areas of the country where the Ehrlichiosis tick disease are common or widespread may be prescribed low doses of antibiotics during tick season.

f) Anaplasmosis: deer ticks and Western blacklegged ticks are carriers of the bacteria that transmit canine Anaplasmosis.

However, there is also another form of Anaplasmosis (caused by a different bacteria) that is carried by the brown deer tick. Because the deer tick also carries other diseases, some animals may be at risk of developing more than one tick-borne disease at the same time.

Signs of Anaplasmosis are similar to Ehrlichiosis and include painful joints, diarrhea, fever, and vomiting as well as possible nervous system disorders.

A dog will usually begin to show signs of Anaplasmosis within a couple of weeks after infection and diagnosis will require blood and urine testing, and sometimes other specialized laboratory tests.

Treatment is with oral antibiotics for up to 30 days, depending on how severe the infection may be. When this disease is quickly treated, most dogs will recover completely, however, subsequent immunity is not guaranteed, which means that a dog may be re-infected if exposed again.

g) Tick Paralysis: is caused when ticks secrete a toxin that affects the nervous system. Affected dogs show signs of weakness and limpness approximately one week after being first bitten by ticks.

Symptoms usual begin with a change in pitch of the dog's usual bark, which will become softer, and weakness in the rear legs that eventually involves all four legs, which is then followed by the dog showing difficulty breathing and swallowing.

If the condition is not diagnosed and properly treated, death can occur. Treatment involves locating and removing the tick and then treating the infected dog with tick anti-serum.

h) Canine Coronavirus: while this highly contagious intestinal disease, which is spread through the feces of contaminated dogs, was first discovered in Germany during 1971 when there was an outbreak in sentry dogs, it is now found worldwide.

This virus can be destroyed by most commonly available disinfectants. Symptoms include:
- Diarrhea
- Vomiting
- Weight loss or anorexia

While deaths resulting from this disease are rare, and treatment generally requires only medication to relieve the diarrhea, dogs that are more severely affected may require intravenous fluids to combat dehydration.

There is a vaccine available, which is usually given to puppies, because they are more susceptible at a young age. This vaccine is also given to show dogs that have a higher risk of exposure to the disease.

i) Leptospirosis: is a disease that occurs throughout the world that can affect many different kinds of animals, including dogs, and as it is also a zoonotic disease, it can affect humans, too. There is potential for both dogs and humans to die from this disease.

The disease is always present in the environment, which makes it easy for any dog to pick up. This is because it is found in many common animals, such as rats, and wildlife, as well as domestic livestock.

Veterinarians generally see more cases of Leptospirosis in the late summer and fall, which is probably because that is when more pets and wildlife are out and about. As well, more cases also occur after heavy rain falls.

The disease is most common in mild or tropical climates around the World, and in the US or Canada, it is more common in states or provinces that receive heavy rainfall.

The good news is that you can protect your dog from leptospirosis by vaccination, and while puppies are not routinely vaccinated against leptospirosis because chances of contracting the disease depends upon the lifestyle of the dog as well as the area in which the dog lives, it makes sense to vaccinate against this disease if you and your dog do live in an area considered a hot spot for leptospirosis, so ask your veterinarian.

City rat populations are a major carrier of leptospirosis.

Cold winter conditions lower the risk because the leptospira organisms do not tolerate the freezing and thawing of near-zero temperatures. They are killed rapidly by drying, but they persist in standing water, dampness, mud and alkaline conditions. Most of the infected wild animals and domestic animals that spread leptospirosis do not appear ill.

The leptospira take up residence in the kidneys of infected animals, which can include rats, mice, squirrels, skunks, and raccoons and when these animals void urine, they contaminate their environment with living leptospira.

Dogs usually become infected after sniffing urine or by wading, swimming or drinking contaminated water that has infected urine in it, and this is how the disease passes from animal to animal. As well, the leptospira can also enter through a bite wound or if a dog eats infected material.

6. Additional Vaccinations

Depending upon where you and your dog live, your veterinarian may suggest additional vaccinations to help combat diseases that may be more common in your area.

7. When Is a Puppy Vaccinated?

The first vaccination needle is normally given to a puppy around six to eight weeks of age, which means that generally it will be the responsibility of the breeder to ensure that the puppy's first shots have been received before their new owner takes them home.

Thereafter, it will be the new puppy's guardians that will be responsible for ensuring that the next two sets of shots, which are usually given three to four weeks after each other, are given by the new guardian's veterinarian at the proper intervals.

8. De-Worming

De-worming kills internal parasites that your dog or puppy may have. The two most common types of worms that may infest your canine companion are round worms and tapeworms, both of which can be passed on to humans.

NOTE: even though your living conditions may be completely sanitary, it is still possible for your dog to have internal parasites because this has nothing to do with where you live or how clean you keep your dog and your home.

It is recommended by the Center for Disease Control (CDC) that puppies be dewormed every 2 weeks until they are 3 months old, and then every month after that, in order to control worms.

Even though puppies are most often regularly wormed by the breeder before the puppies are taken to their forever homes, many veterinarians recommend worming dogs for tapeworm and roundworms every 6-12 months.

The health risk to your puppy or dog includes diarrhea, vomiting, slow growth, and in serious cases causing a bowel blockage or pneumonia, even death.

Most all puppies and dogs will experience worms at some stage in their life and thankfully the problem can be easily and swiftly eliminated with worming medication.

9. Special Care When Pregnant

As canine pregnancy lasts approximately 63 days, and a female will go into labor within 56 to 66 days after becoming pregnant.

Immediately upon noticing signs of pregnancy you will want to take your dog to your veterinarian to confirm the pregnancy and to receive instructions for the proper feeding and care.

During the first days of pregnancy your Beabull may experience morning sickness. Your veterinarian may recommend increasing food intake or adding an egg or cottage cheese to your dog's meals and switching to puppy kibble, which is higher in protein, at around the 30 day mark.

As the female becomes heavier with the puppies, she will lose interest in exercising and her other normal activities and will need to sleep more.

When the time for birthing is drawing near, the female will start to display "nesting" characteristics where she will search for a warm and safe place to give birth. You can help by providing a nesting box and she will likely want to take things into the box to make it more comfortable, such as towels or even a stuffed toy that she will begin to mother.

When the time draws near to whelping, the female may completely lose her appetite and show distress by pacing, panting, and acting uncomfortable. When the birthing time is near, the dog's temperature needs to be checked, and should be around 100.2 to 100.8 degrees Fahrenheit (37.89 to 38.22 degrees Centigrade).

When her temperature drops to approximately 98 to 99.4 degrees Fahrenheit (36.67 to 37.44 degrees Centigrade), the puppies will usually be born within 24 hours.

If you are at all worried about the birthing process you will want to take the mother Beabull immediately to your veterinarian's office.

If all goes well at home, within 5-6 hours of the last puppy's birth, you will need to take the mother and her puppies to your veterinarian for a check up to make sure that she has birthed all puppies and placentas, and that the puppies are all healthy.

10. Licensing

Many cities and jurisdictions around the world require that dogs be licensed.

Usually a dog license is an identifying tag that the dog will be required to wear on their collar. The tag will have an identifying number and a contact number for the registering organization, so that if someone finds a lost dog wearing a tag, the owner of the dog can be contacted.

Most dog tags are only valid for one year, and will need to be renewed annually at the beginning of every New Year, which involves paying a fee, which can vary from jurisdiction to jurisdiction.

From one extreme to the next, owners of dogs living in Beijing, China must pay a licensing fee of $600 (£360), while those living in Great Britain require no fee, because licensing of dogs was abolished in 1987.

Ireland and Northern Ireland both require dogs to be licensed and in Germany dog ownership is taxed, rather than requiring licensing, with higher taxes being paid for breeds of dogs deemed to be "dangerous".

Most US states and municipalities have licensing laws in effect and Canadian, Australian and New Zealand dogs also must be licensed, with the yearly fee approximately $30 to $50 (£18 to £30) depending upon whether the dog has been spayed or neutered.

11. Pet Insurance

Pet guardians commonly ask themselves, when considering medical insurance for their dog, whether they can afford not to have it.

On the one hand, in light of all the new treatments and medications that are now available for our dogs, that usually come with a very high price tag, an increasing number of guardians have decided to add pet insurance to their list of monthly expenses.

On the other hand, some humans believe that placing money into a savings account, in case unforeseen medical treatments are required, makes more sense.

Pet insurance coverage can cost anywhere from $2,000 to $6,000 USD (£1,437 to £4,312) over an average lifespan of a dog, and unless your dog is involved in a serious accident, or contracts a life-threatening disease, you may never need to pay out that much for treatment.

Whether you decide to start a savings account for your dog so that you will always have funds available for unforeseen health issues, or you decide to buy a health insurance plan, most dog lovers will go to any lengths to save the life of their beloved companions.

Having access to advanced technological tools and procedures means that our dogs are now being offered treatment options that were once only reserved for humans.

While some canine conditions that were once considered fatal, are being treated at considerably high expense, even in the face of rapidly increasing costs of caring for our dogs, owners purchasing pet insurance remain a small minority.

In an effort to increase the numbers of people purchasing pet insurance, insurers have teamed with the American Kennel Club and Petco Animal Supplies to offer the insurance, and more than 1,600 companies, such as Office Depot and Google, offer pet insurance coverage to their employees as an optional employee benefit.

Even though you might believe that pet insurance will be your savior anytime your dog needs a trip to the vet's office, you really need to be careful when considering an insurance plan, because there are many policies that contain small print excluding certain ages, hereditary or chronic conditions.

Unfortunately, most people don't consider pet insurance when their pets are healthy because buying pet insurance means playing the odds, and unless your dog becomes seriously ill, you end up paying for something that may never happen. However, just like automobile insurance, you can't buy it after you've had that accident.

For instance, if you take your dog to your veterinarian who discovers that they have something wrong with their eyes, and then you decide to purchase insurance, because you will be required to give the insuring company a history of your dog's health, the eye issue will be part of the history and will likely be excluded from your insurance policy.

In other words, if you're planning on purchasing health insurance for your dog, do it before any problems arise in order to avoid having conditions that may present themselves in the future from being excluded from your policy.

As well, you need to keep in mind that canine health insurance rates will likely increase as your dog becomes older. When your dog is younger, while your policy may only be $17 (£12) per month, it may increase considerably to as much as $170 (£122) or more per month as your dog becomes middle or senior aged, at around 8 to 10 years of age.

Since many of us, in today's uncertain economy, may be hard pressed to pay a high veterinarian bill, generally speaking, the alternative of paying monthly pet insurance premiums will provide peace of mind and improved veterinarian care for our best friends.

Shop around, because as with all insurance policies, pet insurance policies will vary greatly between companies and the only way to know for certain exactly what sort of coverage you are buying is to be holding a copy of that policy in your hand so that you can clearly read what will and what will not be covered.

Don't forget to carefully read the fine print to avoid any nasty surprises, because the time to discover that a certain procedure will not be covered is not when you are in the middle of filing a claim.

Before Purchasing a Policy

There are several considerations to be aware of before choosing to purchase a pet insurance policy, including:
- Is your dog required to undergo a physical exam?
- Is there a waiting period before the policy becomes active?
- What percentage of the bill does the insurance company pay — after the deductible?
- Are payments limited or capped in any way?
- Are there co-pays (cost to you up front)?
- Does the plan cover pre-existing conditions?
- Does the plan cover chronic or recurring medical problems?
- Can you choose any vet or animal hospital to treat your pet?
- Are prescription medications covered?
- Are you covered when traveling with your pet?
- Does the policy pay if your pet is being treated and then dies?

When you love your dog and worry that you may not have the funds to cover an emergency medical situation that could unexpectedly cost thousands, the right pet insurance policy will provide both peace of mind and better health care for your beloved fur friend.

12. Identifying and Finding Lost Dogs

a) Micro-Chipping: this implant is a very small integrated circuit, approximately twice the size of a grain of rice, enclosed in glass that is implanted underneath the dog's skin (or other animal) with a syringe.

The chip uses passive Radio Frequency Identification (RFID) technology, and is also known as a PIT tag (Passive Integrated Transponder).

The microchip is usually implanted, without anesthetic, into the scruff of a dog's neck by a veterinarian or shelter and has no internal power source, which means that they must be read by a scanner or *"interrogator"* which energizes the capacitor in the chip, which then sends radio signals back to the scanner so that the identifying number can be read.

Manufacturers of microchips often donate scanners to animal shelters and veterinarian clinics and hospitals.

While many communities are proposing making micro-chipping of all dogs mandatory, such as N. Ireland, and micro-chipping is a requirements for any dogs traveling to the state of Hawaii, many others are not especially pleased with this idea because they believe it's just more big business for little reward.

For instance, while approximately one quarter of European dogs have a microchip implant, the idea is definitely lacking in popularity in the United States, where only 5% of dogs are micro-chipped.

Even though micro-chipping is used by animal shelters, pounds, animal control officers, breeders and veterinarians, in order to help return a higher percentage of lost canines to their owners, some of the resistance to this idea can be explained by inherent problems with the ability of some organizations to correctly read the implants.

As an example, if the scanner is not tuned to the same frequency as the implanted microchip, it will not be read, which renders the process useless.

Pet microchips are manufactured with different frequencies, including 125 kHz, 128 kHz and 134.2 kHz. While approximately 98% of the pet microchips in the US use 125 kHz, those in Europe use 134.2 kHz.

In other words, if the facility reading your dog's microchip does not have a compatible scanner, your dog will not be identified and returned to you. Further, what may turn out to be worse than the scanner incompatibility problem could be increasing evidence to indicate that microchips might cause cancer.

As well, some microchips will migrate inside the dog's body and while they may start out in the dog's neck, they could end up in their leg or some other body part.

You will have to weigh information known about microchips, including possible cancer risks, and the odds of losing your dog against whether or not a microchip is something you want to have for your Beabull.

Whether or not you choose a microchip for your dog, generally the cost ranges between $25 and $50 (£18 and £36) depending on what your veterinarian may charge for this service.

NOTE: as of 6th April 2017, it is mandatory for those owning dogs in the UK to have them micro-chipped.

b) Tattooing: dogs are tattooed to help identify them in case they are lost or stolen. Many dog guardians prefer this safe, simple solution to micro-chipping because there is no need to locate a scanner that reads the correct frequency and there are no known side effects.

Because a tattoo is visible, it is immediately recognizable and reported when a lost dog is found, which means that tattooing could easily be the most effective means of identification available.

As well, dog thieves are less likely to steal a dog that has a permanent visible form of identification. There are several registries for tattooed dogs, including the National Dog Tattoo Registry in the UK, which has a network of Accredited Tattooists across the UK. The fee for tattooing and registering a dog for their lifetime may average $43 (£31).

In the United States, the National Dog Registry (NDR) was founded in 1966 and since then, NDR has supervised, directed, conducted, or overseen the tattooing of more than 6 million animals.

The cost for tattooing a single dog is approximately $10 (£7), and you will also have to pay a one-time registration fee of approximately $45 (£32).

c) Pet Trackers: in today's electronic world, many people are wondering if a Pet Tracker might be a good idea for helping to keep their beloved canine safe. So, what exactly are Pet Trackers, how much do they cost, how do they work and how do you know which one to choose? First of all, you need to know that there are many in the marketplace and that there are basically two categories comprised of (1) Cellular GPS Trackers and (2) Radio Trackers, which are a special collar attached to your dog.

A GPS Tracker can help you locate your dog in real time by utilizing cellular towers and requires the use of a SIM card or some sort of cellular service, with average pricing ranging from $100 (£72) to $300 (£216).

Radio Trackers, which have been used for decades, utilize what some may consider outdated technology and are often used for hunting dogs, functioning over a limited range, much like a "Walkie Talkie". The more you spend for a Radio Tracker, the greater the range will be and pricing can range from $200 (£144) to $1,000 (£719).

d) Where to Look: if your dog goes missing, there are many places you can contact and steps you can take that may help you locate your lost dog, including:
   • Retracing your dog's last known location;
   • Contacting your friends and neighbours;
   • Putting up flyers on telephone poles throughout your neighbourhood, with your contact details and a photograph of your dog;
   • Calling all local shelters and pounds every day;
   • Contacting local rescue organisations;
   • Contacting your breeder;
   • Contacting local schools - children might have seen your dog in their neighbourhood;
   • Distributing flyers with a photograph of your dog and your contact details in all neighbourhood stores and businesses;
   • Contacting all businesses that deal with lost pets;
   • Posting a picture on your Facebook or other social media;
   • Asking your local radio station for help;
   • Advertising in your local newspaper.

13. Yearly Cost of Ownership
It can be difficult to accurately estimate what the cost of owning every Beabull might be because there are too many variables and unexpected medical problems, which might arise that may not otherwise be considered average. For instance, you may like to buy fancy clothes, new collars and

leashes every year, the latest toys and gadgets, or the most expensive food for your dog every week that might also not be considered average.

However, when thinking about sharing your life with a dog, it's important to consider more than just the daily cost of feeding your dog.

Many humans do not think about whether or not they can truly afford to care for a dog before they bring one home, and not being prepared can cause stress and problems later on. Remember that being financially responsible for your dog is a large part of being a good guardian.

Beyond the initial investment of purchasing your Beabull puppy from a reputable breeder, for most guardians, owning a dog will include the costs associated with the following:

- Food
- Treats
- Pee pads, poop bags, potty patches
- Leashes and collars
- Safety harnesses
- Travel kennels or bags
- House training pens
- Clothing
- Toys
- Beds
- Professional grooming or equipment
- Shampoo and conditioner
- Neutering or spaying
- Regular veterinary care
- Obedience or dog whispering classes
- Pet sitting, walking or boarding
- Pet insurance
- Tattooing
- Micro-chipping
- Yearly licensing
- Unexpected emergencies

As you can see from the list above, there are many variables involved in being a canine guardian that may or may not apply to your particular situation.

For instance, depending upon where you shop, what type of food and how much you feed your dog, what sort of veterinarian or grooming care you choose, whether or not you have pet insurance and what types of items you purchase for your dog's well being, the yearly cost of owning a Beabull could be estimated at anywhere between $700 and $3,000 (£503 and £2,156) per year.

Other contributing factors that may have an effect on the overall yearly cost of owning a Beabull can include the region where you live, the weather, the accessibility of the items you need, your own lifestyle preferences and your dog's age and individual needs.

NOTE: another interesting fact that may influence the overall cost associated with caring for a particular breed of dog is, according to a recent study of 2,000 dogs, closely related to what breed of dog you may be sharing your home with.

According to a recent article written by Sarah Griffiths and published in the Daily Mail on June 13, 2014, there is now a list of the top ten most *"destructive"* purebred dog breeds.

This interesting study was carried out in reference to damage a dog may cause by ripping up the carpet, chewing through the fence, destroying the plants in the garden, eating the remote or your most expensive shoes, etc.

Of course, all us humans expect some degree of damage from our furry friends during their lifetime, however, sometimes it can be quite a surprisingly large amount when you begin to add up the total amounts spent on cleaning, replacing and repairing damaged property, and the amount can be even higher if your dog becomes involved in destroying the neighbor's property, too.

The prize for the top ten destroyers is awarded to the cute and tiny Chihuahua, with average repair costs totaling $1,468 (£1,055) over the dog's lifetime, followed by the Dachshund, Boxer, Dalmatian, Bulldog, Great Dane, Husky, Beagle, Pointer and German Shepherd.

On the other hand, the top ten least destructive breeds, in descending order, include such candidates as the Staffordshire Bull Terrier, causing a reported $302 (£217) of damage over the dog's lifetime, followed by the West Highland White Terrier, Yorkshire Terrier, Spaniel, Whippet, Shih Tzu, Golden, Jack Russell, Rottweiler and Sheepdog.

With all the cross breeding and creation of hybrid, designer canines these days, there are some very interesting studies being carried out, such as this one, that will help us humans better understand our favorite companions and what we may be letting ourselves in for.

NOTE: the more popular a particular breed may be, and the more positive traits a particular breed may enjoy will also make the cost of initially purchasing a puppy from a breeder more costly.

14. Your Dog and the Law
You may not be aware that there are many laws in place around the world regarding out of control or dangerous dogs, that have serious consequences, including heavy fines and/or jail time for the dog's guardian.

For instance, the government of the United Kingdom (and other countries) have legislated strict controls regarding all dogs and it's against the law for any dog to be dangerously out of control, no matter where they are.

Make sure that you are up do date with respect to controlling your dog in public, in private or even in your own home.

Chapter 12: Grooming

You will want to get your Beabull puppy used to the routine of grooming early on, so that they will not be traumatized for the rest of their life, every time grooming is necessary.

Not taking the time to regularly involve your puppy in grooming sessions could lead to serious, unwanted behavior that may include trauma to your dog, not to mention stress or injury to yourself in the form of biting and scratching, that could result in a lifetime of unhappy grooming sessions.

When you neglect regular, daily or at least a weekly at home grooming session with your puppy or dog to remove dead hair and check toenails, this will not only cost you and your canine companion, in terms of possible trauma it may also cost you in veterinarian fees should you not be aware of a problem that could have been discovered early on during regular grooming sessions.

An effective home regimen will include not just surface brushing, but also getting to all those sensitive areas easily missed around the ears and collar area, the armpit area, and the back end and tail.

Do not allow yourself to get caught in the *"my dog doesn't like it"* trap, which is an excuse many owners will use to avoid regular grooming sessions.

When you allow your dog to dictate whether they will permit a grooming session, you are setting a dangerous precedent that could lead to a lifetime of trauma for both you and your dog.

When humans neglect daily grooming routines, many dogs develop a heightened sensitivity, especially with regard to having their legs and feet held, their ears inspected, or their nails clipped, and will do anything they can to avoid the process when you need to groom them.

Make a pact with yourself right from the first day you bring your Beabull puppy home, never to neglect a regular grooming routine and not to avoid sensitive areas, such as regular brushing, trimming toenails or brushing teeth, just because your dog may not particularly *"like"* it.

Remember that a few minutes of regular grooming sessions each day with your dog is also a wonderful opportunity for closely bonding.

1. Bath Time

Step One: before you get your dog anywhere near the water, it's important to make sure that you brush out any debris, dead hair, mats or tangles from their coat before you begin the bathing process.

As well, removing any debris or mats from your dog's coat beforehand will make the entire process easier on both you, your dog, and your drains, which will become clogged with dead hair if you don't remove it beforehand.

Step Three: whether you're bathing your Beabull in your bathtub or shower, you will always want to first lay down a rubber bath mat to provide a more secure footing for your dog and to prevent your tub or sink from being scratched.

Step Four: have everything you need for the bath (shampoo, conditioner, sponge, towels) right next to the tub or in the shower, so you don't have to go searching once your dog is already wet.

TIP: place cotton balls in your dog's ear canals to prevent accidental splashes from entering the ear canal that could later cause an ear infection.

Step Five: if using a tub, fill it with four to six inches of lukewarm water (not too hot as dogs are more sensitive to hot water than us humans) and put your dog in the water. Completely wet your dog's coat right down to the skin by using a detachable showerhead. If you don't have a spray attachment, a cup or pitcher will work just as well.

TIP: no dog likes to have water poured over its head and into its eyes, so use a wet sponge or wash cloth to wet the head area.

Step Six: apply shampoo as indicated on the bottle instructions by beginning at the head and working your way down the back. Be careful not to get shampoo in the eyes, nose, mouth or ears. Comb the shampoo lather through your dog's hair with your fingers, making sure you don't miss the areas under the legs and tail.

Step Seven: after allowing the shampoo to remain in your dog's coat for a couple of minutes, thoroughly rinse the coat, right down to the skin with clean, lukewarm water using the spray attachment, cup or pitcher. Comb through your dog's coat with your fingers to make sure all shampoo residue has been completely rinsed away.

TIP: any shampoo remaining in a dog's coat will lead to irritation and itching. Once you've rinsed, take the time to rinse again, especially in the armpits and underneath the tail area. Use your hands to gently squeeze all excess water from your dog's coat.

Step Eight: apply conditioner as indicated on the bottle instructions and work the conditioner throughout your dog's coat. Leave the conditioner in your dog's coat for two minutes and then thoroughly rinse again with warm water, unless the conditioner you are using is a *"leave-in"*, no-rinse formula.

NOTE: The best conditioner for will contain mink oil, which adds a gloss to deepen and enrich the natural color of the coat.

It is also a good idea to choose a brand of conditioner that contains sunscreen to help protect from ultraviolet radiation when your dog is outside on sunny days.

Applying a good conditioner containing protein to your dog's coat after bathing will help to rebuild, restructure and protect the coat by bonding to the shaft of each individual hair. Pull the plug on your tub and let the water drain away as you use your hands to squeeze excess water from your dog's legs and feet.

Step Nine: immediately out of the water, wrap your puppy or dog in dry towels so they don't get cold and use the towels to gently squeeze out extra water before you allow them to shake and spray water everywhere.

Unless it's a warm day out, you will want to dry him or her right away with your hand held hairdryer and be careful not to let the hot air get too close to their skin.

TIP: you can use your hand or a soft brush or comb to lift and fluff the coat to help it dry more quickly, and you will want to place your hand between the hairdryer and your dog's hair so that they will never get a direct blast of hot air and never blow air directly into their face or ears, and don't forget to remove the cotton balls from their ears.

2. Ear Care

There are many ear cleaning creams, drops, oils, rinses, solutions and wipes formulated for cleaning your dog's ears that you can purchase from your local pet store or veterinarian's office.

You may prefer to use a home remedy that will just as efficiently clean your dog's ears, such as Witch Hazel or a 50:50 mixture of hydrogen peroxide and purified water.

TIP: if you are going to make your own ear cleaning solution, find a bottle with a nozzle, measure your solution, properly diluted and mixed into the bottle, and use your preparation to saturate a cotton makeup remove pad to wipe out the visible part of your dog's ears. Always make sure the ears are totally dried after cleaning.

3. Eye Care

Every dog should have their eyes regularly wiped with a warm, damp cloth to remove build up of daily secretions in the corners of the eyes that can be unattractive and uncomfortable for the dog as the hair becomes glued together.

If this build up is not removed every day, it can quickly become a cause of bacterial yeast growth that can lead to eye infections. When you take a moment every day to gently wipe your dog's eyes with a warm, moist cloth, you will help to keep your dog's eyes comfortable and infection free.

4. Nail Care

Allowing your dog to have long, untrimmed nails can result in various health hazards including infections or an irregular and uncomfortable gait that can result in damage to their skeleton.

Although most dogs do not particularly enjoy the process of having their nails trimmed, and most humans find the exercise to be a little scary, regular nail trimming is a very important grooming practice that should never be overlooked. When you get them used to having their nails trimmed at a young age, they will quietly tolerate the process for the rest of their life.

In order to keep your adult Beabull's toenails in good condition and the proper length, you will need to purchase a medium or large-size plier type nail trimmer at a pet store and learn how to correctly use it.

Generally speaking, if you can hear your dog's nails clacking or scratching on the floor or road surface when they walk, their nails are too long, and if you continue to allow your dog's nails to be too long, the nail quick will grow longer into the nail, which will make it more difficult to keep them trimmed to the correct length.

NOTE: when your Beabull is a small puppy, it will be best to trim their nails with a pair of nail scissors, which you can purchase at any pet store, that are smaller and easier to use on puppy nails. All you need to do is snip off the curved tip of each nail.

Further, if you want your dog's nails to be smooth, without the sharp edges clipping alone can create, you will also want to invest in a toenail file or a special, slow speed, rotary Dremel™ trimmer, equipped with a sanding disk, which is designed especially for dog nails.

Some dogs will prefer the rotary trimmer to the squeezing sensation of the nail clipper and when you keep your dog's nails regularly trimmed, the Dremel™ may be the only tool you will ever need.

NOTE: never use a regular shop Dremel™ tool on a dog's toenails as it will be too high speed and will burn your dog's toenails. Only use a slow speed Pet Nail Grooming tool specifically designed for dog nails.

5. Dental Care

As a conscientious Beabull guardian you will need to regularly care for your dog's teeth throughout their entire life.

a) Retained Primary Teeth: often a young dog will not naturally lose their puppy or baby teeth without intervention from a licensed veterinarian.

Therefore, keep a close watch on your puppy's teeth around the age of 6 or 7 months of age to make certain that the baby teeth have fallen out and that the adult teeth have space to grow in.

If your puppy has not naturally lost all their baby teeth, any remaining teeth will need to be pulled, in order to allow room for the adult teeth to properly grow in, and the best time to do this will be at the same time they visit the veterinarian's office to be spayed or neutered.

b) Periodontal Disease: please be aware that 80% of three-year-old dogs suffer from periodontal disease and bad breath because their guardians do not look after their dog's teeth. What makes this shocking statistic even worse is that with simple, daily care, it is possible to entirely prevent canine gum disease and bad breath.

The pain associated with periodontal disease will make your dog's life miserable, as it will be painful for them to eat and the associated bacteria can infect many parts of the dog's body, including the heart, kidney, liver and brain, all of which they will have to suffer in silence.

If your dog has bad breath, this could be the first sign of an unhealthy mouth and gum disease caused by plaque build-up on the teeth.

As well, if your dog is drooling excessively, this may be a symptom secondary to dental disease. Your dog may be experiencing pain or the salivary glands may be reacting to inflammation from excessive bacteria in the mouth. If you notice your dog drooling, you will want to have them professionally examined at your veterinarian's office.

c) Teeth Brushing: slowly introduce your dog to teeth brushing early on in their young life so that they will not fear it.

Begin with a finger cap toothbrush when they are young puppies, and then move to a soft bristled toothbrush, or even an electric brush, as all you have to do is hold it against the teeth while the brush does all the work. Sometimes with a manual brush, you may brush too hard and cause the gums to bleed.

Never use human toothpaste or mouthwash on your dog's teeth because dogs cannot spit and human toothpaste that contains toxic fluoride will be swallowed. There are many flavored dog toothpastes available at the pet store or veterinarian's office.

Also, it's a good idea to get your dog used to the idea of occasionally having their teeth scraped or scaled, especially the back molars which tend to build up plaque. Be very careful if you are doing this yourself because the tools are sharp.

TIP: if you need help keeping your dog's mouth open while you do a quick brush or scrape, get yourself a piece of hard material (rubber or leather) that they can bite down on, so that they cannot fully close their mouth while you work on their teeth.

When your Beabull is a young puppy, take the time to get them used to having their mouth handled and your fingers rubbing their teeth and gums.

Next, buy some canine toothpaste at your local pet store specially flavored to appeal to dogs and apply this to your dog's teeth with your finger. Then slowly introduce the manual or electric toothbrush to your dog. When you go slowly, they will get used to the buzzing and vibrating of the electric brush, which will do a superior job of cleaning their teeth.

First, let them see the electric brush, then let them hear it buzzing, and before you put it in their mouth, let them feel the buzzing sensation on their body, while you move it slowly toward their head and muzzle.

When your dog will allow you to touch their muzzle while the brush is turned on, the next step is to lift their lip and quickly brush a couple of teeth at a time until they get used to having them all brushed at the same time.

Always happily praise them for allowing you to brush their teeth, especially when they are first getting used to the idea.

TIP: another simple home solution for helping to keep your dog's breath fresh and their teeth white is Bicarbonate of Soda (baking soda). Simply sprinkle some into a dish and dip your finger or toothbrush first in water and then into the Bicarbonate of Soda. Then use this to clean your dog's teeth and massage their gums. Some dogs seem to object less to this procedure when you use your finger.

Whether you let the electric toothbrush do the work for you, or you are using your finger or a manual toothbrush, make certain that you brush in a circular motion and when using a brush, angle the bristles so that they extend underneath the gums to help prevent plaque buildup, gum disease and loose teeth.

d) Teeth Scaling: use of a tooth scraper or scaling tool once or twice a month can help to remove plaque buildup. Most accumulation will be found on the outside of the teeth and on the back molars, near the gum line.

Go slowly and carefully because these tools are sharp and only do this when your dog is calm and relaxed, a little bit at a time.

e) Healthy Teeth Tips: despite what most dog owners might put up with as normal, it is <u>not</u> normal for your dog to have smelly dog breath or canine halitosis.

Bad breath is the first sign of an unhealthy mouth, which could involve gum disease or tooth decay. The following tips will help keep your dog's mouth and teeth healthy:

Hydrogen Peroxide – keep your dog's teeth sparkling white and their breath fresh by using old-fashioned hydrogen peroxide as your doggy toothpaste. Hydrogen peroxide is what's in the human whitening toothpaste. There will be such a small amount on the brush that it will not harm your dog, and will kill any bacteria in your dog's mouth.

Toothpaste – many canine toothpastes are formulated with active enzymes to help keep tartar build-up at bay.

Plaque and Halitosis – help prevent tooth plaque and doggy halitosis by feeding your dog natural, hard bones at least once a month, which will also help to remove tartar while polishing and keeping their teeth white.

Bones – feed large bones so there is no danger of swallowing, and do NOT boil the bones first because this makes the bone soft (which defeats the purpose of removing plaque), and boiling could cause bones to splinter into smaller pieces that could create a choking or puncturing hazard for your dog.

Dental Chews – feed a daily dental chew or hard biscuit to help to remove tartar while exercising the jaws and massaging the gums. Some dental chews contain natural breath freshening cinnamon, cloves or chlorophyll.

Coconut Oil – helps to prevent smelly dog breath while giving your dog's digestive, immune and metabolic functions a boost at the same time. Dogs love the taste, so add ¼ teaspoon to your dog's dinner and their breath will soon be much sweeter.

Teeth Brushing – keep your dog's mouth comfortable and healthy by getting into the habit of brushing their teeth every night before bedtime.

6. Skin Care

Keeping your dog's coat clean by regularly bathing with canine shampoo and conditioner and free from mats, debris and parasites, as well as providing plenty of clean water and feeding them a high quality diet free from allergy-causing ingredients will go a long way toward keeping their skin healthy and itch-free and their coat shiny and healthy looking.

Between bath times, there are many moist doggy wipes on the market that are especially formulated with the correct pH balance to help keep your dog clean and their skin healthy. Consider getting into the habit of wiping down your dog with one of these moist towels every night before bed.

7. Pest Control

a) Fleas: every dog usually picks up a flea or two sometime in their lifetime, so you should be prepared for this inevitability by ensuring that you have a good flea shampoo on hand as well as a flea comb.

If you notice your dog biting, scratching or chewing at his or herself, the chances that they have picked up a flea or two is quite high, so it's time for a flea bath.

b) Ticks: if your dog goes roaming freely through wooded and bushy areas with large trees, they may also pick up the occasional tick.

Always carefully check through your dog's coat and ears after they have been romping through the woods, and make sure that you also have a solution on hand that will kill a tick or the proper tool that can easily and safely twist any size of tick out of a dog's skin.

A very effective product, which is 100% safe for humans and animals, that will kill ticks on contact, is a natural pest control product made by CedarCide called *"Best Yet Organic Bug Spray"*.

As well, ticks can be quickly and easily removed with a simple to use *"Tick Twister"*.

8. Brushing

An often over looked task, that is a necessary part of maintaining the health of a Beabull, is daily brushing.

As well, taking time to brush your dog's coat will also give you an opportunity to bond with your fur friend, while identifying any problems (such as fatty lumps or bumps and matted hair) early on, before they may become more serious.

Make sure that your grooming sessions are as pleasant as possible by choosing the right tools for your dog's type and length of coat.

You will need minimal brushes to keep your dog's coat in good condition, including a bristle brush. As well as one or two brushes, and perhaps a chamois for wiping down a dusty coat, it's always a good idea to invest in a flea comb (just in case).

9. Equipment Required

A stiff **bristle brush** can be used to help remove debris and dead hair from the coat and also to help distribute natural oils to keep the coat looking healthy and shiny.

Flea combs, as the name suggests, are designed for the specific purpose of removing fleas from a dog's coat. A flea comb is usually small in size for maneuvering in tight spaces, and may be made of plastic or metal with the teeth of the comb placed very close together to trap hiding fleas.

A **Tick Twister**, is a simple device for painlessly, easily and quickly removing ticks that have imbedded themselves in your dog's skin.

Nail clippers or scissors (and/or a slow speed pet Dremel™) will be tools you need to use every couple of weeks or more, depending on how quickly your dog's nails grow and what types of surfaces they may be walking on.

10. Products

Shampoos: NEVER make the mistake of using human shampoo or conditioner for bathing your dog because dogs have a different pH balance than humans.

For example, shampoo for humans has a pH balance of 5.5, whereas shampoo formulated for our canine companions has an almost neutral pH balance of 7.5. Any shampoo with a lower pH balance will be harmful to your dog because it will be too harshly acidic for their coat and skin, which can create skin problems.

Always purchase a shampoo for your dog that is specially formulated to be gentle and moisturizing on your dog's coat and skin, that will not strip the natural oils, and which will nourish your dog's coat to give it a healthy shine.

As a general rule, make sure that you read the instructions provided on the shampoo bottle, and avoid shampoos containing insecticides or harsh chemicals.

TIP: if your dog is suffering from an infestation of fleas, you may want to bathe them with shampoo containing pyrethrum (a botanical extract found in small, white daisies) or a shampoo containing citrus or tea tree oil, or bath and spray them with the very effective CedarCide products which can also be used to spray down their bedding and any carpets in the home.

Conditioners: while many of us humans use a conditioner after we shampoo our own hair, a large number of canine guardians forget to use a conditioner on our own dog's coat after bathing.

Even if the bathing process is one that you wish to complete as quickly as possible, you will want to reconsider this little oversight because, just as conditioning our human hair improves its condition, the same is true for our dog's coat.

Conditioning your dog's coat will not only make it look and feel better, conditioning will also add additional benefits, including:

- Preventing the escape of natural oils and moisture
- Keeping the coat cleaner for a longer period of time
- Repairing a coat that has become damaged or dry
- Restoring a soft, silky feel
- Helping the coat dry more quickly
- Protection from the heat of the dryer and breakage of hair

Unless you are using a two-in-one shampoo plus conditioner, spend the extra two minutes to condition your Springer Spaniel's coat after bathing. The benefits of doing so will be appreciated by both yourself and your dog that will have overall healthy skin and a coat with a natural shine.

Styptic Powder: you will always want to avoid causing any pain when trimming your dog's toenails, because you don't want to destroy their trust in you regularly performing this necessary task.

However, accidents do happen, therefore if you accidentally cut into the vein in the toenail, know that you will cause your dog pain, and that the toenail will bleed. Therefore, it is always a good idea to keep some styptic powder (often called *"Kwik Stop")* in your grooming kit.

Dip a moistened finger into the powder and apply it, with pressure, to the end of the bleeding nail because this is quickest way to stop a nail from bleeding in just a few seconds.

TIP: if you do not have styptic powder available, there are several home remedies that can help stop the bleeding, including a mixture of baking soda and cornstarch, or simply cornstarch alone. Also, a cold, wet teabag or rubbing with scent-free soap can also be effective. These home remedies will not be as instantly effective as styptic powder.

Ear Powders: which can be purchased at any pet store, are designed to help keep your dog's ears dry while at the same time inhibiting the growth of bacteria that can lead to infections. Ear powders are also used when removing excess hair growth from inside a dog's ear canal as the powder makes it easier to grip the hair.

Ear Cleaning Solutions: your local pet store will offer a wide variety of ear cleaning creams, drops, oils, rinses or wipes specially formulated for cleaning your dog's ears. As well, there are also many home remedies that will just as efficiently clean your dog's ears without the high price tag.

NOTE: because a dog's ears are a very sensitive area, always read the labels before purchasing products and avoid any solutions that list alcohol as the main ingredient.

Home Ear Cleaning Solutions: the following are three effective home solutions that will efficiently clean your dog's ears:

Witch Hazel is a natural anti-inflammatory that works well to cleanse and protect against infection while encouraging faster healing of minor skin traumas.

A 50:50 solution of **Organic Apple Cider Vinegar and Purified Water** has been used as an external folk medicine for decades. This mixture is a gentle and effective solution that kills germs while naturally healing.

A 50:50 solution of **Hydrogen Peroxide and Purified Water** is useful for cleansing wounds and dissolving earwax.

Whatever product you decide to use for cleaning your dog's ears, always be careful about what you put into your dog's ears and thoroughly dry them after cleaning.

Skin Folds: you will also want to clean wrinkles and skin folds every day to prevent an build-up of bacteria that can lead to infections.

Canine Toothpastes: when it comes time to brush a dog's teeth, this is where many guardians fail miserably, often using the excuse that *"my dog doesn't like it"*.

Whether they like it or otherwise is not the issue, because in order to keep your dog healthy, they <u>must</u> have healthy teeth and the only way to ensure this, is to brush their teeth every day.

The many canine toothpastes on the market are usually flavored with beef or chicken in an attempt to appeal to the dog's taste buds, while others may be infused with mint or some other breath freshening ingredient in an attempt to appeal to humans by improving the dog's breath.

Honestly, your dog is not going to be begging for you to brush his or her teeth no matter how tasty the paste might be, therefore, effectiveness, in the shortest period of time, will be more of a deciding factor than whether or not your dog prefers the taste of the toothpaste.

Some dog toothpastes contain baking soda, which is the same mild abrasive found in many human pastes, and is designed to gently scrub the teeth. However, just how much time you will have to spend scrubbing your dog's teeth, before they've had enough, may be too minimal to make these pastes very effective.

Other types of canine toothpastes are formulated with enzymes that are designed to work chemically by breaking down tartar or plaque in the dog's mouth. These pastes do not need to be washed off your dog's teeth and are safe for them to swallow. Whether or not they remain on the dog's teeth long enough to do any good might be debatable.

TIP: old-fashioned hydrogen peroxide cleans while killing germs and keeping teeth white. Just dip your dog's toothbrush in a capful of hydrogen peroxide, shake off the excess, and brush their teeth. There will be such a small amount in your dog's mouth that you don't need to worry about them swallowing it.

Paw Creams: depending on activity levels and the types of surfaces our canine counterparts usually walk on, they may suffer from cracked or rough pads. You can restore resiliency and keep your dog's paws in healthy condition by regularly applying a cream or lotion to protect their paw pads and a good time to do this is just after you have clipped their nails.

NOTE: if you live in a hot climate, be aware that sidewalks, road surfaces and sandy beaches can get extremely hot for your dog's feet. As well, because a dog is that much closer to hot surfaces, this means that on a hot day, they will be feeling the effects of being heated from both sides. If you live in a very hot climate, choose to walk them during the cooler hours of the day, or walk them in shaded or grassy areas only.

Organic Pest Control: CedarCide is a company that makes 100% safe, organic products to control biting bugs on your fur friends without worrying about harmful chemicals that are not good for you, your children or your canine companions.

Simply spray it on, and bugs of any sort that come into contact with the solution will be dead, while your dog's coat will be shiny and fresh smelling, like the inside of a cedar chest.

11. Professional Grooming

The best way to find a groomer is to ask others who they use and whether they are happy with the results.

An average price for professionally bathing and grooming a dog may vary greatly depending on where you live and prices can increase depending upon the size of the dog, the type and condition of their coat, how calmly they accept the procedure, and whether the salon is also trimming nails or expressing anal glands.

Chapter 13: Socializing

Most Beabull will be naturally friendly and social dogs that enjoy interacting with humans and other dogs. However, they will still need to be exposed to different people, places and unfamiliar sights and sounds when they are puppies so that they do not learn to be nervous or anti-social.

Much of how any dog behaves will depend entirely upon you, how extensively they were socialized as a puppy and how much they are continually being socialized throughout their life.

Never make the mistake of thinking that you only need to socialize a young puppy and then they will be fine for the rest of their life, as all dogs require constant socializing and once they reach adolescence, their personality can really begin to assert itself.

All dogs need to be exposed to different people, dogs, places and unusual sights and sounds when they are puppies and throughout their adult life.

Any dog that is not regularly socialized may become shy or suspicious of unfamiliar or unusual people or circumstances, which could lead to nervous or fearful behavior, which can then lead to aggression.

1. With Other Dogs and Pets

Generally speaking, the majority of an adult dog's habits and behavioral traits will be formed between the ages of birth and one year of age.

Keep in mind that the Beagle side of this hybrid mix may mean that any offspring may retain a strong prey drive for chasing smaller animals, such as squirrels, birds or the neighbor's cat and they may not be totally trustworthy around other smaller family pets.

This is why it will be very important to introduce your puppy to a wide variety of locations, sights, sounds, smells and situations during the most formative period in their young life, which is usually the first 16 weeks.

Your puppy will learn how to behave, in all these various circumstances, by following your lead, feeling your energy and watching how you react in every situation.

For instance, never accidentally reward your puppy or dog for displaying nervousness, fear or growling at another dog or person by picking them up.

Picking up a puppy or dog at this time, when they are displaying unbalanced energy, actually turns out to be a reward for them, and you will be teaching them to continue with this type of behavior.

As well, picking up a puppy places them in a top dog position, where they have the higher ground and literally (because they are higher up) become more dominant than the person or dog they may have just growled at.

The correct action to take in such a situation is to gently correct your puppy, with a firm, yet calm energy by distracting them with a "no", or a quick sideways snap of the leash to get their attention back on you, so that they learn to let you deal with the situation on their behalf.

If you allow a fearful, nervous or shy puppy deal with situations that unnerve them without your direction, they may learn to react with fear or aggression to unfamiliar circumstances and you will have created a problem that could escalate into something more serious as they grow older.

The same is true of situations where a young puppy may feel the need to protect itself from a larger or older dog that may come charging in for a sniff. It is the guardian's responsibility to protect the puppy so that they do not feel that they must react with fear or aggression in order to protect themselves.

Once your puppy has received all their vaccinations, you can take them out to public dog parks and various locations where many dogs and people are found.

Before allowing them to interact with other dogs or puppies, take them for a disciplined walk on leash so that they will be a little tired and less likely to immediately pounce excitedly on all other dogs.

Keep your puppy on leash and close beside you, because most young puppies are a bundle of out of control energy, and you need to protect them while teaching them how far they can go before they may get themselves into trouble with adult dogs that might not appreciate their excited playfulness.

Remember that they may not have experienced the company of other dogs since you brought them home, and now that they have completed their course of vaccinations, they will understandably be excited and perhaps a little hesitant about seeing dogs again.

Keep a close watch on your Beabull puppy to make sure they are not being overwhelmed by too many other dogs, or getting overly excited and stressed or nervous, because it is your job to protect your puppy.

Remember that this hybrid tends to play bit too aggressively and this type of behavior will need to be firmly curtailed at a young age. If your puppy shows any signs of aggression or domination toward another puppy, dog or person, you must immediately step in and calmly discipline them, otherwise by doing nothing, you will be agreeing with their behavior and will be allowing them to get into situations that could become serious behavioral issues as they grow in age and size.

No matter the age or size of your puppy, allowing them to display aggression or domination over another dog or person is never a laughing matter and this type of behavior must be immediately curtailed.

2. With Other People

Take your puppy everywhere with you and introduce them to many different people of all ages, sizes and ethnicities. This will be easy to do, because most people will automatically be drawn to you when they see you have a puppy because few humans can resist stopping to say hello to a cute puppy.

Most humans will want to interact with your puppy and if they ask to hold him or her, this is a good opportunity to socialize your puppy and show them that humans are friendly.

Do not let others (especially young children) play roughly with your puppy or squeal at them in a high-pitched voices because this can be very frightening for a sensitive young puppy, or can cause them to be overly excited and this is when they may resort to using their teeth during play.

Even though this dog is usually very patient with children, you do not want to teach your puppy that humans are a source of crazy, excited energy.

Be especially careful when introducing your puppy to young children who may accidentally hurt your puppy, because you don't want your dog to become fearful of children as this could lead to aggression issues later on in life. Explain to children that your puppy is very young and that they must be calm and gentle when playing or interacting in any way.

3. Within Different Environments

It can be a big mistake not to take the time to introduce your Beabull puppy to a wide variety of different environments because when they are not comfortable with different sights and sounds, this could cause them possible trauma later in their adult life.

Be creative and take your puppy everywhere you can imagine when they are young so that no matter where they travel, whether strolling along a noisy city sidewalk or beside a peaceful shoreline, they will be equally comfortable.

Do not make the mistake of only taking your new puppy into areas where you live and will always travel because they need to also be comfortable visiting areas you might not often visit, such as noisy construction sites, airports or a shopping area across town.

Your puppy needs to see all sorts of sights, sounds and situations so that they will not become fearful should they need to travel with you to any of these areas.

Your puppy will take their cues from you, which means that when you are calm and in control of every situation, they will learn to be the same because they will trust your lead.

For instance, take your puppy to the airport where they can watch people and hear planes landing and taking off or take them to a local park where they can see a baseball game, or for a stroll beside a schoolyard at recess time when noisy children are out playing, or to the local zoo or farm and let them get a close up look at horses, pigs and ducks.

Again, never think that socialization is something that only takes place when your dog is a young puppy, as proper socialization, is ongoing for your dog's entire life.

4. Loud Noises

Many dogs can show extreme fear of loud noises, such as fireworks or thunderstorms.

When you take the time to desensitize your Beabull to these types of noises when they are very young, it will be much easier on them during stormy weather or holidays such as Halloween or New Year's when fireworks are often a part of the festivities.

You can purchase CD's that are a collection of unusual sounds, such as vacuums or hoovers, airplanes, people clapping hands, screaming children, and more, that you can play while working in your kitchen or relaxing in your living room or lounge.

When you play these sounds and pretend that everything is normal, the next time your puppy or dog hears these types of sounds elsewhere, they will not become upset or agitated because they have learned to ignore them.

TIP: bubble wrap is also another simple way to desensitize a dog that is fearful of popping sounds. Show them the bubble wrap, pop a few of the cells and if they do not run away, give them a treat. You can start with the bubble wrap that has small, quieter cells, and then graduate them to the larger celled (louder) bubble wrap.

Also make sure that you get your young puppy used to the sounds of thunder and fireworks at an early age because these types of shrieking, crashing, banging and popping sounds of fireworks or thunder as well as the high pitched beeping of household smoke and fire alarms can be so traumatic and unsettling for many dogs, that sometimes, no matter how much you try to calm your dog, or pretend that everything is fine, there is little you can do.

Some dogs literally lose their minds when they hear the loud popping or screeching noises of fireworks and alarms and start running or trying to hide and you cannot communicate with them at all.

Make sure that your dog cannot harm itself trying to escape from these types of noises, and if possible, calmly hold them until they begin to relax.

If your dog loses it's mind when it hears these types of noises, simply avoid taking them anywhere near fireworks and if at times when they might hear these noises going off outside, play your inside music or TV louder than you might normally, to help disguise the exterior noise of fireworks or thunder.

Some dogs will respond well to wearing a *"ThunderShirt"* which is specifically designed to alleviate anxiety or trauma associated with loud rumbling, popping or banging noises. The idea behind the design of the ThunderShirt is that the gentle pressure it creates is similar to a hug that, for some dogs, has a calming effect.

There are also sonic collars you can have your dog wear that plays calming music that eliminates stressful ultra-high and low end frequencies that cause dogs to become stressed.

Do not underestimate the importance of taking the time to continually (not just when they are puppies) socialize and desensitize your puppy to all manner of sights, sounds, individuals and locations because to do so will be teaching them to be a calm and well balanced member of your family that will quietly follow you in every situation.

Chapter 14: Training

1. Trainability

As the Beabull has two often stubborn and independent-minded parents, while they are usually mild-mannered and eager to please, they will almost undoubtedly display some of these similar, headstrong traits.

What the dog thinks: *"I smell food – forget about the walk, give me the food!"*

While even-tempered and devoted to their humans, during training this dog's guardian will need to exercise patience in combination with a firm, yet kind hand. For best results, positive reinforcement, by adding the incentive of training treats will go a long way toward helping to ensure an interested participant.

This hybrid is totally capable of learning basic commands and hand signals and you should begin this as soon as you bring them home. Short training sessions that include food rewards will work best for this puppy, and once they get a little older, you can increase training times and add in fun exercises such as a game of fetch, a few tricks or a puzzle to help stimulate the mind and keep him or her interested.

The Beabull will be happy with a couple of walks each day, and some time to play freely at the local dog park, or perhaps a game of fetch with the children in your back yard.

Since many dogs that were previously working breeds have been relegated to the role of house pet, you need to consider activities, beyond a walk around the block, which are both excellent for your dog and fun for you, such as:

Further, depending on the particular dog, and how active their humans may be, this dog may enjoy running an Agility course or participating in Flyball, Frisbee or Barn Hunt sports.

This dog loves to spend time with their humans, and when taught with positive reinforcement, despite their often stubborn streak, the Beabull will usually be an eager participant who can learn to excel at anything their humans have the time and patience to teach.

Every dog is an opportunist. This means that any training sessions need to somehow benefit them so that they learn that performing certain tasks will reap them a reward or benefit that they want. In the case of the Beabull, this will usually include treat rewards.

For instance, if your dog has developed an unwanted behavior, rather than by reacting to it, which is still the dog getting your attention, even if it is negative attention, you must then teach him or her, in a positive way, what to do that does not involve them repeating the unwanted behavior.

What you can teach them depends entirely upon the time and patience you have to devote to their education.

No matter what you decide to teach your dog, always train with patience and kindness and NEVER yell, hit or punish a dog during training, or at any time for that matter. Using harsh, mean or loud training methods could frighten any dog and cause them to shut down.

As well, any sort of harsh treatment could cause your fur friend to lose trust and respect of you, and they could also learn to fear you, which is NOT the type of relationship you want to have with your dog.

All training sessions should be happy and fun filled with plenty of rewards and positive reinforcement, which will ensure that your dog is an excellent student who looks forward to learning new commands and tricks.

2. Puppy Training Basics

Most humans believe that they need to take their young dog to puppy classes, and generally speaking, this is a good idea for any young Beabull (after they have completed all their vaccinations), because it will help to get them socialized.

Beyond puppy classes for socializations reasons, hiring a professional dog whisperer for personalized private sessions to train the humans may be far more valuable than training situations where there are multiple dogs and humans together in one class as this can be very distracting for everyone concerned.

a) Choosing a Discipline Sound: choosing a *"discipline sound"* that will be the same for every human family member will make it much easier for your puppy to learn what they can or cannot do and will be very useful when warning your puppy before they engage in unwanted behavior.

The best types of sounds to get a dog's attention are short and sharp that you and your family members can quickly say and so that the sound will immediately get the attention of your puppy because you want to be able to easily interrupt them when they are about to make a mistake.

It doesn't really matter what the sound is, so long as it gets your dog's attention and everyone in the family is consistent. A sound that is very effective for most puppies and dogs is a simple *"UH"* sound said sharply and with emphasis.

Most puppies and dogs respond immediately to this sound and if caught in the middle of doing something they are not supposed to be doing will quickly stop and give you their attention or back away from what they were doing.

b) Three Most Important Words: "Come", "Sit" and "Stay" will be the three most important words you will ever teach your puppy. These three basic commands will ensure that your Beabull remains safe in almost every circumstance.

For instance, when your puppy correctly learns the "Come" command, you can always quickly bring them back to your side if you should see danger be approaching.

When you teach your puppy the "Sit" and "Stay" commands you will be further establishing your leadership role. A puppy that understands that their human guardian is their leader will be a safe and happy follower.

All that's necessary for effectively teaching your puppy their basic first commands is a calm, consistent approach, combined with your endless patience.

Many puppies are ready to begin training at about 10 to 12 weeks of age, however, be careful not to overdo it when they are less than four to six months of age, as their attention span will be short.

Make your training sessions no more than 5 or 10 minutes, positive and pleasant with lots of praise and/or treats so that your puppy will be looking forward to their next session.

COME: while most puppies will be capable of learning commands and tricks at a young age, the first and most important command you need to teach your puppy is the recall, or *"Come"* command.

Begin the "Come" command inside your home. Go into a larger room, such as your living room area. Place your puppy in front of you and attach their leash or a longer line to their Martingale collar, while you back away from them a few feet.

Say the command "Come" in an excited, happy voice and hold your arms open wide, which is the hand signal. If they do not immediately come to you, gently give a tug on the leash so that they understand that they are supposed to move toward you. When they come to you praise them and give a treat they really enjoy.

Once your puppy can accomplish a "Come" command almost every time inside your home, you can then graduate them to a nearby park or quiet outside area where you will repeat the process.

You may want to purchase an extra long, lightweight line (25 or 50 feet) so that you are always attached to your puppy and can encourage them in the right direction should they become distracted.

SIT: the "Sit" and "Stay" commands are both easy commands to teach that will help to keep your puppy safe and out of danger in almost every circumstance.

Find a quiet time to teach these commands when your puppy is not overly tired. Ask your puppy to "Sit" and if they do not yet understand the command, show them what you mean by gently squeezing with your thumb and middle finger the area across the back that joins with their back legs.

Do not just push them down into a sit as this can cause damage to their back or joints. When they sit, give them a treat and praise them.

When you say the word "Sit", at the same time show them the hand signal for this command.

While you can use any hand signal, the universal hand signal for "Sit" is: Right arm (palm open facing upward) parallel to the floor, and then raising your arm, while bent at the elbow toward your right shoulder.

Once your puppy is sitting reliably for you, remove the verbal "Sit" and replace it with the hand signal.

It's important to begin teaching hand signals during the adolescent stage of your puppy's life, because this will also help them to be more attentive and communicate in a way that is more natural for a dog — by watching you and feeling your energy, rather than always having to hear you speak a command.

Every time you take your dog out for a walk, which is often a cause of excitement, get into the habit of asking them to sit quietly and patiently while you put on their leash — then ask them to sit and calmly wait while you put on your shoes or jacket.

After you approach the door, ask them to sit again while you open the door — again after you are on the other side of the door — ask them to sit while you lock the door.

When you are methodical and deliberate and take your time with this, your dog will be able to connect the dots and will soon learn the new routine of being patient and paying attention to you.

If there are stairs or landings involved, ask them to sit at the top and also again at the bottom.

Every time you arrive at street intersection or a crosswalk, ask your puppy to sit again, and do this in reverse when coming back home. Also, every time you stop during your walk to speak to a neighbor, greet a friend or admire the view, ask your puppy to sit.

Every time you ask your young dog to sit for you, they are learning several things all at once — that they must remain calm while paying attention to you, that you are the boss and that they must look to you for direction and respect you as their leader.

Also, a sitting puppy is much more easy to control than one standing at the alert, ready to bolt out the door or jump on someone. As well, because the action of sitting helps to calm the mind of an excited puppy (or dog), teaching your puppy the "Sit" command is a very important part of their daily interactions with your family members as well as people you may meet when out on a walk.

When you ask your puppy to "Sit" before you interact in any way with them, before you go out or in every door, before you feed them, etc., you are helping to quiet their mind, while teaching them to look to you for direction, and at the same time making it more difficult for them to jump, lunge or disappear out a door.

STAY: once your puppy can reliably "Sit", say the word "Stay" and hold your outstretched arm, palm open toward their head and back away a few steps.

If they try to follow, calmly say "No" and put them back into "Sit". Give a treat and then say again, "Stay" with the hand signal and back away a few steps.

Once your puppy is sitting and staying, you can then ask them to "Come". Don't forget to use the open arms hand signal for "Come." Be a little excited with the "Come" command so that your puppy will always enjoy correctly responding and immediately returning to you.

Practice these three basic commands everywhere you go, and use the "Sit" command as much as you can to ensure its success rate.
As your puppy gets older, and their attention span increases, you will be able to train for longer periods of time.

The hand signal for "stay" is: right arm fully extended toward your dog's head, palm open, hand bent up at the wrist.

TIP: if you are right-handed, use your right arm and hand for the signal, and if you are left-handed, use your left arm and hand for the signal. Using your dominant hand will be much more effective because your strongest energy emanates from the palm of your dominant hand.

3. Beginner Leash Lesson

Equipment Required: 4 or 6-foot leash, Martingale training collar.

The most important ongoing bonding exercise you will experience with your new puppy is when you go out for your daily walks together.

Far, far too many people ignore this critical, multi-tasking time that is not only important for your puppy's exercise, it fulfills a multitude of their needs, including:
  - Exercising their body
  - Fulfilling their natural roaming urges
  - Teaching them discipline, which engages their mind

- Learning to follow, trust and respect you
- Reinforcing that you are their leader

As soon as you bring your new puppy home you will want to teach them how to walk at your side while on leash without pulling.

Every time your puppy needs to go out to relieve his or herself, slip on their collar and snap on that leash.

At first your puppy may struggle or fight against having a collar around their neck, because the sensation will be new to them. However, at the same time they will want to go with you, so exercise patience and encourage them to walk with you.

Be careful never to drag them, and if they pull backward and refuse to walk forward with you, simply stop for a moment, while keeping slight forward tension on the leash, until your puppy gives up and moves forward. Immediately reward them with your happy praise, and if they have a favorite treat, this can be an added incentive when teaching them to walk on their leash.

Always walk your puppy on your left side with the leash slack so that they learn that walking with you is a relaxing experience. Keep the leash short enough so that they do not have enough slack to get in front of you.

If they begin to create tension in the leash by pulling forward or to the side, simply stop moving, get them back beside you, and start over.

Be patient and consistent with your puppy and very soon they will understand exactly where their walking position is and will walk easily beside you without any pulling or leash tension.

Remember that walking with a new puppy is an exciting experience for them as they will want to sniff everything and explore their new world, so give them lots of understanding and don't expect them to be perfect all the time.

When your puppy is very young, and wanting to put everything in their mouths, walk them in a harness AND collar and leash, so that you can have a second leash attached to the harness.
All puppies want to put everything in their mouths, therefore, when they are wearing a collar and leash, AND a harness and leash, you will be able

to easily lift them over cigarette butts or other garbage you may encounter while out walking.

Once they grow out of the habit of tasting all manner of garbage, you can dispense with the harness and second leash.

4. Surviving Adolescence

The adolescent period in a young Beabull's life, between the ages of 6 and 12 months, is the transitional stage of both physical and psychological development when they are physically almost full grown in size, yet their minds are still developing and they are testing their boundaries and the limits that their human counterparts will endure.

This can be a dangerous time in a puppy's life because this is when they start to make decisions on their own which, if they do not receive the leadership they need from their human guardians, can lead to developing unwanted behaviors.

Learning how to make decisions on their own would be perfectly normal and desirable if your puppy were living in the wild, amongst a pack of dogs, because learning to make decisions would be necessary for their survival.

However, when living within a human environment, your puppy must always adhere to human rules and it will be up to their human guardians to continue their vigilant, watchful guidance in order to make sure that they do.

Many humans are lulled into a false sense of security when their new puppy reaches the age of approximately six months, because the puppy has been well socialized, they have been to puppy classes and long since been house trained.

The real truth is that the serious work is only now beginning and the humans and their new puppy could be in for a time of testing that could seriously challenge the relationship and leave the humans wondering if they made the right decision to share their home with a dog.

If the human side of the relationship is not prepared for this transitional time in their young dog's life, their patience may be seriously tried, and the relationship of trust and respect that has been previously built can be damaged, and could take considerable time to repair.

While not all adolescent puppies will experience a noticeable adolescent period of craziness, because every puppy is different, most young dogs do commonly exhibit at least some of the usual adolescent behaviors, including reverting to previous puppy behaviors.

Some of these adolescent behaviors might include destructive chewing of objects they have previously shown no interest in, selective hearing or ignoring previously learned commands, displaying aggressive behavior, barking uncontrollably, jumping on everyone, barking at everything that moves, or reverting to relieving themselves in the house, even though they were house trained months ago.

Keeping your cool and recognizing these adolescent signs is the first step toward helping to make this transition period easier on your puppy and all family members.

The first step to take that can help keep raging hormones at bay, is to spay or neuter your puppy just prior to the onset of adolescence, at around four or five months of age.

While spaying or neutering a puppy will not entirely eliminate the adolescent phase, it will certainly help and at the same time will spare your puppy the added strain of both the physical and emotional changes that occur during sexual maturity.

As well, some female puppies will become extremely aggressive toward other dogs during a heat, and non-neutered males may become territorially aggressive and pick fights with other males.

Once your puppy has been spayed or neutered, you will want to become more active with your young dog, both mentally and physically by providing them with continued and more complex disciplined exercises.

This can be accomplished by enrolling your adolescent Beabull in a dog whispering session or more advanced training class, which will help them to continue their socialization skills while also developing their brain.

Even though it may be more difficult to train during this period, having the assistance of a professional and continuing the experience of ongoing socialization amongst other dogs of a similar size can be invaluable, as this is the time when many young dogs begin to show signs of antisocial behavior with other dogs as well as unknown humans.

When your dog is provided with sufficient daily exercise and continued socialization with unfamiliar dogs, people and places that provides interest and expands their mind, they will be able to transition through the adolescent stage of their life much more seamlessly.

5. Releasing Energy

The adolescent period in any puppy's life is a time of boundless energy. Excess energy will be even more apparent in an intelligent, high energy puppy and you will need to find ways to safely allow them to release this energy every day.

Since most humans cannot walk nearly fast enough to accommodate the needs of an energetic puppy, you will first want to walk your Beabull beside you on leash, and then find a safe place where they can run off leash, either chasing a ball, retrieving a Frisbee or playing and running in an enclosed area with other similar sized dogs where you can always supervise.

6. The Unruly Adolescent

If your puppy happens to be especially unruly during their adolescent phase, you will need to simply provide them with more outlets for safely exercising and releasing their energy while limiting their opportunities for making mistakes.

For instance, a puppy who is digging up the yard, or chewing up just about anything they can get their teeth on will need to be closely supervised so that you can direct their energy into less harmful pursuits.

It does absolutely no good to yell at your puppy for engaging in behavior you are not happy with, and in fact, yelling or getting angry will only desensitize your young dog from listening to any of your commands.

Although you may eventually get the results you want, if you yell loud enough, your puppy will then be reacting out of fear, rather than respect, and this will be damaging to your relationship.

Displaying calm, yet assertive energy is the ONLY energy that works well to help your adolescent puppy understand what is required of them.

All other human emotions (frustration, anger, impatience, sadness, excitement) are "read" by puppies and dogs as being unstable, and not only will the smart and sensitive Beabull not understand these emotions, they will not respect you for displaying these types of unstable energies.

An extremely rambunctious adolescent dog may need to have their free run of the house curtailed so that they are confined to areas where you can easily supervise them.

Make sure they are within eyesight at all times, so that if they do find an opportunity to make a mistake, you can quickly show them what is permitted and what is not.

Adolescence may also be a time when you might have to insist that your young companion sleeps in their crate with the door closed whenever you cannot supervise, as well as at bedtime so they continue to understand that you have firm rules.
As well, keeping on top of house training is also a good idea during the adolescent period of your puppy's life because some adolescent puppies may become stubborn and forget that they are already house trained.

This means actually taking the time to be involved in the process by leashing up your pup and physically taking them outside whenever they need to relieve themselves.

Many times humans that have back yards tend not to be very involved in the housebreaking routine because they just open a door and let their dogs run free in the back yard.

Too many humans with convenient yards simply do not participate at all in the bathroom routine of their young dogs and thereby miss out on endless opportunities to reinforce who is the boss.

7. Rewarding Unwanted Behavior

Often humans make the mistake of accidentally rewarding unwanted behaviors.

It is very important to recognize that any attention paid to an overly excited, out of control, adolescent puppy, even negative attention, is likely going to be rewarding for your puppy. Therefore, when you engage with an out of control puppy, you end up actually rewarding them, which will encourage them to continue more of this unwanted behavior.
Be aware that chasing after a puppy when they have taken something they are not supposed to have, picking them up when they are barking or showing aggression, pushing them off when they jump on you or other

people, or yelling when they refuse to come when called, are all forms of attention that can actually be rewarding for most puppies.

As your dog's guardian, it will be your responsibility to provide calm and consistent structure for your puppy, which will include finding acceptable and safe ways to allow your puppy to vent their energy without being destructive or harmful to property, other dogs, humans, or the actual puppy.

Activities that create or encourage an overly excited puppy, such as rough games of tug-o-war, wild games of chase through the living room, or overly aggressive or excited play sessions with another dog or puppy, should be immediately curtailed, so that your adolescent puppy learns how to control their energy and play quietly and appropriately without jumping on everyone or engaging in barking or mouthy behavior.

Further, if your adolescent puppy displays excited energy simply from being petted by yourself, your family members or any visitors, you will need to teach yourself, your family and your friends to ignore your puppy until they calm down. Otherwise, you will be inadvertently teaching your puppy that the touch of humans means excitement.

For instance, when you continue to engage with an overly excited puppy or dog, you are rewarding them for out of control behavior and literally teaching them that when they see humans, you want them to display excited energy.

Even worse, once your puppy has learned that humans are a source of excitement, you will then have to work very long and hard to reverse this behavior.

Children are often a source of excitement that can cause an adolescent puppy to be extremely wound up.

Do not allow your children to engage with an adolescent Beabull puppy unless you are there to supervise and teach the children appropriate and calm ways to interact with the puppy.

In order to keep everyone safe, it is very important that your puppy learn at an early age that neither children nor adults are sources of excitement. You can help develop the mind of an adolescent dog and the minds of growing children at the same time by teaching children that your puppy needs structured walks and by showing them how to play fetch, search, hide and seek, or how to teach the puppy simple tricks and obedience skills that will be fun and positive interaction for everyone.

8. Back to "Sit" Basics

When your puppy is going through what could be a belligerent and trying adolescence, when it seems that they have forgotten everything they may have already previously learned, this is an especially good time to revisit the simple "Sit" command.

Now, in order to help re-establish your leadership role, you will want to ask your puppy to sit at every opportunity because the simple act of "sitting" will help to calm an excited mind and will get your puppy's focus back on you.

Every time you take your dog out for a walk, which is often a cause of excitement, get into the habit of asking them to sit quietly and patiently while you put on their leash — then ask them to sit and calmly wait while you put on your shoes or jacket.

After you approach the door, ask them to sit again while you open the door — again after you are on the other side of the door — ask them to sit while you lock the door.

When you are methodical and deliberate and take your time with this, your dog will be able to connect the dots and will soon learn the new routine of being patient and paying attention to you.

If there are stairs or landings involved, ask them to sit at the top and also again at the bottom. Every time you arrive at street intersection or a crosswalk, ask your puppy to sit again, and do this in reverse when coming back home.

Also, every time you stop during your walk to speak to a neighbor, greet a friend or admire the view, ask your puppy to sit. Every time you ask your young dog to sit for you, they are learning several things all at once — that they must remain calm while paying attention to you, that you are the boss and that they must look to you for direction and respect you as their leader.

Also, a sitting puppy is much more easy to control than one standing at the alert, ready to bolt out the door or jump on someone.

Once your puppy is reliably sitting for you at least 50% of the time with voice command, also include the hand signal for "Sit", so that they will hear the word and also see the signal.

While you can use any hand signal, the universal hand signal for "Sit" is: Right arm (palm open facing upward) parallel to the floor, and then raising your arm, while bent at the elbow toward your right shoulder. Once your dog is sitting reliable for you, remove the verbal "Sit" and replace it with the hand signal.

It's important to begin teaching hand signals during the adolescent stage of your puppy's life, because this will also help them to be more attentive and communicate in a way that is more natural for a dog — by watching you and feeling your energy, rather than always having to hear you speak a command.

As well, because the action of sitting helps to calm the mind of an excited puppy (or dog), teaching your puppy the "Sit" command is a very important part of their daily interactions with your family members as well as people you may meet when out on a walk.

When you ask your puppy to "Sit" before you interact in any way with them, before you go out or in every door, before you feed them, etc., you are helping to quiet their mind, while teaching them to look to you for direction, and at the same time making it more difficult for them to jump, lunge or disappear out a door.

The adolescent stage in a young dog's life is the perfect time to begin teaching hand signals for all your common commands, because they must look at you to understand what is expected of them, and when they are looking at you, they are more focused and less likely to take matters into their own paws.

9. Giving Up is Not an Option

Too often we humans get frustrated and give up on our dogs when they change from being the cute, cuddly and mostly obedient little puppy they once were, and become all kinds of trouble you never bargained for, as they grow into their adolescent stage.

Often times, it will be during the confusing adolescent stage of a dog's life that they find themselves abandoned and behind bars as their humans who promised to love and protect them, leave their once loved fur friend at the local pound or SPCA.

First of all, not all dogs go through a crazy adolescent period, and secondly, even if they do, please read this section carefully humans, because you can live through puppy adolescence and come out the other side relatively unscathed and a much more knowledgeable and patient guardian.

Congratulations are in order because you've been successful with potty training your young puppy and with teaching them to sleep in their own kennel at night.

Further, you've lived through the teething troubles, the chewing and the hand nipping and you no longer have to get up at 3:00 a.m. to let your puppy out to go potty.

As well, you've taught your puppy their first few basic commands, and socialized them with many other dogs, people and places, so you should feel proud of all your accomplishments and the leaps and bounds you and your puppy have accomplished together over the last several months.

Even though your adolescent puppy may be starting to act like a Tasmanian devil, and you may be having second thoughts, now is not the time to give up on them and yourself just because it may seem like someone switched your dog when you weren't looking.

Now is the time to remain calmly consistent and persistent, and to know that you will eventually be able to enjoy the happy rewards that all those months of diligent puppy training have brought to your relationship.

Yes, it can be quite a shock when what used to be your well behaved little darling who never chewed anything they weren't supposed to suddenly takes it into their head to eat all the tassels off your Persian rug or chew through a seat belt in your vehicle during the short 15 minutes you were shopping.

Even more disconcerting might be when your previously obedient and loving puppy, who always listened to your directions, suddenly appears to have gone deaf and can't remember their name when you call them to follow you inside the house, and instead they take off running after a cat three blocks away.

And then, what happened to that quiet little puppy that never appeared to have a mean bone in their body that now spends most of their time at the window barking and growling at everything and everyone passing by?

Welcome to the world of canine adolescence where it appears that your puppy has turned into some sort of monster and all your previous hard work was for nothing. This is the time when your patience may be seriously tested.

Of course, this dramatic switch from being the world's best puppy into the monster you can no longer control is not true for all puppies, as every puppy is unique.

However, being prepared for the worst will help you ride any impending storm and get you both safely out the other side where you can enjoy an even closer relationship than you previously had.

The adolescent phase may be very subtle for your puppy or on the other hand, it may be so dramatic that you're starting to feel guilty every time you drive past the local SPCA or dog pound because thoughts of rehoming are running through your head.

If you are at the stage with your puppy that you are having great difficulties and wondering if you made the right decision to share your home with a dog, rest assured that puppy adolescence is a normal phase of their development, which can be managed, and which will definitely pass.

As well, if you are finding yourself totally overwhelmed, there are many professionals who can provide valuable assistance to help you through this stage of your puppy's development.

For most puppies, adolescence will begin between the ages of five and seven months and this is also the time that you need to be making an appointment at your veterinarian's office to have your puppy spayed or neutered.

Although neutering or spaying will not prevent undesirable adolescent behavior entirely, it can certainly reduce the intensity of it, as during this period there are hormonal changes occurring that will affect your puppy's behavior.
While it's usually hormones that are the major cause of behavioral changes in your adolescent puppy, there are also physical changes occurring at the same time that you may not be aware of.

For instance, your puppy will be going through physical growth spurts which might be causing them some pain, as well as changes related to growth in their brain while your puppy's cerebral cortex becomes more involved in thinking for itself.

Usually, during this time of brain growth, a puppy will be trying to make choices for themselves, and may or may not yet be capable of making the right choices. This is why their behavior can appear to be quite erratic.

During the early adolescent period of brain development in your Beabull puppy, the signals sometimes get mixed up and rerouted, which can result in the perplexing responses you might notice, when for instance, you ask you puppy to sit and they stare dumbly at you, even though they learned this command months ago.

Don't worry because so long as you remain calm and consistent, your previous training will return.

10. Re-visit Puppy Training Basics

All that's necessary for effectively teaching your puppy their basic first commands is a calm, consistent approach, combined with your endless patience.

Many puppies are ready to begin training at about 10 to 12 weeks of age, however, be careful not to overdo it when they are less than four to six months of age, as their attention span will be short.

Make your training sessions no more than 5 or 10 minutes, positive and pleasant with lots of praise and/or treats so that your puppy will be looking forward to their next session.

Also, introduce the hand signals that go along with the verbal commands so that once they learn both, you can remove the verbal commands in favor of just hand signals.

Return to Puppy Training Basics and go over the "Come", "Sit" and "Stay" commands and use them every day, in every opportunity to help your young dog progress through their unpredictable adolescent period.

11. Basic Hand Signals
Hand signal training is by far the most useful and efficient training method for every dog, including the Beabull. This is because all too often we

inundate our canine companions with a great deal of chatter and noise that they really do not understand because English is not their first language.

Contrary to what some humans might think, the first language of a Beabull, or any dog, is a combination of sensing energy and watching body language, which requires no spoken word or sound.

Therefore, when we humans take the time to teach our dog hand signals for all their basic commands, we are communicating with them at a level they instinctively understand, plus we are helping them to become a focused follower, as they must watch us to understand what is required of them.

a) COME Hand Signal: you can kneel down for this command or stay standing. Open your arms wide like you are hugging a very large tree. This hand signal can be seen from a long distance.

When first teaching hand signals to your dog, always show the hand signal for the command at the same time you say the word.

If they are totally ignoring the command, it will be time to incorporate a light lunge line, which is a very long leash to help you teach the "Come" command.

Simply attach a 20-foot line to their collar and let them sniff about in a large yard or at your neighborhood park, then at your leisure, firmly ask them to "Come" and show the hand signal. If they do not immediately come to you, give a firm tug with the lunge line, so that they understand what you are asking of them.

If they still do not "Come" toward you, simply reel them in until they are in front of you. Then let them wander about again, until you are again ready to ask them to "Come".

Repeat this process until your dog responds correctly at least 80% of the time. You can also reinforce the command by giving a treat when they come back to you when asked. It is important to make sure that returning to you is always a fun, pleasant and rewarding experience for your dog or puppy. Always ask them to "Sit" when they return to you and then praise them enthusiastically.

NOTE: the "Come" command is *THE* most important command you will ever teach your dog, therefore, <u>never</u> ask them to come to you if you are angry or upset or to punish them in any way, because you want them to be solid with this command, and never fear coming when called.

b) SIT Hand Signal: right arm (palm open facing upward) parallel to the floor, and then raise your arm, while bent at the elbow toward your shoulder.

Sit is a very simple, yet extremely valuable command for all puppies and dogs.

If your dog is not sitting on command, try holding a treat above and slightly behind their head, so that when they look up for it they may automatically sit in order to see the treat they want. Slowly remove the treat as reward and replace the treat with a "life reward", such as a chest rub or a scratch behind the ears and your happy smile.

If your dog is not particularly treat motivated, lift up and slightly back on the leash when asking them to sit (stand in front of them), and if they still are having difficulties, reach down with your free hand, place it across your dog's back at the place where the back legs join the hip and gently squeeze.

Remember -- Do NOT simply push down on your dog's back to force their hind legs to collapse under them as this pressure could harm their spine or leg joints.

c) STAY Hand Signal: right armed fully extended toward your dog's head, palm open, hand bent up at the wrist.

Once your dog is in the "Sit" position, ask them to "Stay" with both the verbal cue and the hand signal.

TIP: if you are right-handed, use your right arm and hand for the signal, and if you are left-handed, use your left arm and hand for the signal. Using your dominant hand will be much more effective because your strongest energy emanates from the palm of your dominant hand.
While your dog is sitting and staying, slowly back away from them. If they move from their position, calmly put them back into Sit and ask them to "Stay" again, using both the verbal cue and the hand signal.

Continue to practice this until your dog understands that you want them to stay sitting and not move toward you.

With all commands, when your dog is just learning, be patient and always reward them with a treat and your happy praise for a job well done.

12. Simple Tricks

When teaching your Beabull tricks, in order to give them extra incentive, find a treat that they really like, and give the treat as a reward and to help solidify a good performance.

Most dogs will be extra attentive during training sessions when they know that they will be rewarded with their favorite treats.

If your puppy is less than six months old when you begin teaching them tricks, keep your training sessions short (no more than 5 or 10 minutes) and fun, and as they become adults, you can extend your sessions as they will be able to maintain their focus for longer periods of time.

a) Shake a Paw: who doesn't love a dog that knows how to shake a paw? This is one of the easiest tricks to teach any dog.

TIP: most dogs are naturally either right or left pawed. If you know which paw your dog favors, ask them to shake this paw.

Find a quiet place to practice, without noisy distractions or other pets, and stand or sit in front of your dog. Place them in the sitting position and have a treat in your left hand. Say the command *"Shake"* while putting your right hand behind their left or right paw and pulling the paw gently toward yourself until you are holding their paw in your hand. Immediately praise them and give them the treat.

Most dogs will learn the "Shake" trick quite quickly, and very soon, once you put out your hand, your dog will immediately lift their paw and put it into your hand, without your assistance or any verbal cue.

Practice every day until they are 100% reliable with this trick, and then it will be time to add another trick to their repertoire.
b) Roll Over: you will find that just like your dog is naturally either right or left pawed, that they will also naturally want to roll either to the right or the left side. Take advantage of this by asking your dog to roll to the side they naturally prefer.

Sit with your dog on the floor and put them in a lie down position. Hold a treat in your hand and place it close to their nose without allowing them to grab it, and while they are in the lying position, move the treat to the right or left side of their head so that they have to roll over to get to it.

You will very quickly see which side they want to naturally roll to, and once you see this, move the treat to this side. When they roll over to this side, immediately give them the treat and praise them.

You can say the verbal cue *"Over"* while you demonstrate the hand signal motion (moving your right hand in a circular motion) or moving the treat from one side of their head to the other with a half circle motion.

Once your dog can roll over every time you ask, it will be time to teach them another trick.

c) Sit Pretty: while this trick is a little more complicated, and most dogs pick up on it very quickly, remember that every dog is different so always exercise patience.

Find a quiet space with few distractions and sit or stand in front of your dog and ask them to "Sit". Have a treat nearby (on a countertop or table) and when they sit, use both of your hands to lift up their front paws into the sitting pretty position, while saying the command *"Sit Pretty"*. Help them balance in this position while you praise them and give them the treat.

Once your dog can do the balancing part of the trick quite easily without your help, sit or stand in front of your dog while asking them to *"Sit Pretty"* and hold the treat above their head, at the level their nose would be when they sit pretty.

TIP: when first beginning this trick, place your dog beside a wall so they can use the wall to help them balance.

If they attempt to stand on their back legs to get the treat, you may be holding the treat too high, which will encourage them to stand on their back legs to reach it. Go back to the first step and put them back into the *"Sit"* position and again lift their paws while their backside remains on the floor.

Sit Pretty Hand Signal: hold your straight arm, fully extended, over your dog's head with a closed fist.

Make this a fun and entertaining time for your dog and practice a few times every day until they can *"Sit Pretty"* on hand signal command every time you ask.

A young Beabull puppy should be able to easily learn these basic tricks before they are six months old and when you are patient and make your training sessions short and fun for your dog, they will be eager to learn more.

13. Adult Training

The Beabull who is guided by an experienced guardian should be able to teach this hybrid many different commands, tricks and sports. Therefore, in order to ensure a happy and healthy companion that remains a healthy weight, make sure that you get them involved in as much activity as possible, including advanced training or canine sports.

When your dog is a full grown adult (approximately two years of age), you will definitely want to begin more complicated or advanced training sessions. They will enjoy the attention and when you have the desire and patience, you may be surprised at how much this dog can learn.

For instance, you may wish to teach your adult dog more advanced tricks, such as how to dance, or the opposite sided paw shakes or rollovers, which are more difficult than you might expect.

If you and your dog are really enjoying learning new tricks together, you might want to advance to teaching them the hand signals for *"commando crawl"*, how to *"speak"* or to *"jump through the human hoop"*, or perhaps get them involved in a fun sport.

All of these tricks and many more are fun to teach and will exercise both your dog's mind and body by taking advantage of their natural ability to excel as a working breed dog. As well, the more control you have over your dog, the easier it will be to teach them a fun sport, such as Agility or Dock Diving.

The only restriction to how far you can go with training your adult Beabull will be your imagination and their personal ability or desire to perform.

14. Behavioral Issues

It can be difficult, if not impossible to generalize or speculate with respect to alleviating possible behavioral issues or problems you may encounter with your dog because, in most cases, a dog suffering from behavioral issues requires the assistance of a dog whisperer or dog psychologist.

When reading anything about how to prevent or cure behavioral issues, please be aware that behavioral problems most often cannot be properly assessed or cured by reading a book. The reason for this is because there are just too many variables and unique situations, individual dogs, individual humans, unique circumstances, and endless reasons why they may have developed any particular behavioral issue.

Therefore, without knowing the dog's particulars and all the history of what has transpired between the dog and his or her guardian that came before or how the problem might have manifested itself, attempting to write about how to cure a particular issue will be no more than a best guess.

This is why someone whose dog is suffering from a specific behavioral issue that is in turn, at the least embarrassing, or at the worst dangerous, and driving the humans and the entire neighborhood crazy, must be properly addressed by engaging the services of a competent, professional dog whisperer (psychologist or behaviorist) who can ask many questions, properly assess the situation and then design a unique plan for alleviating the problem.

15. Overheating
a) Outside: be very careful, when training or walking this heavily coated dog outside during hot weather, so that you do not allow them to become overheated. When it's warm outside, always carry water with you to help keep them hydrated.

TIP: if your dog has a coat that is darker colored, you can easily help to keep them cooler on hot, sunny days by having them wear a light weight vest that is a lighter color than their own coat because this will help to deflect the heat.

Remember that dogs are close to heated pavement, road surfaces or sandy beaches, which means that on a hot, sunny day, they will literally be heated from both the bottom and the top.

If the surface is very hot, do not allow them to walk on it. Instead, exercise them during cooler morning or evening hours or take them to a grassy or shaded area.

b) Inside Vehicles: never leave your dog alone inside a vehicle on a warm day, even for a few minutes.

On a warm, summer day that may seem a pleasant 72°F to us humans (22.2 Celsius), inside a metal vehicle, the temperature can quickly climb to 120°F (48.8 Celsius), even with the windows left open, in a short ten minutes.

In many parts of the world it is a crime to leave a dog unattended inside a vehicle and you may return to find that your window has been broken and your dog rescued by local authorities that may have intervened, or much more serious and tragic, you may return to find that your dog has died from heat exhaustion.

As well, you might think that leaving the windows cracked and parking underneath a tree that is providing shade will be good enough for your dog. Think again, because dogs are not as efficient as humans when it comes down to regulating their body temperature and they could seriously suffer while you're off shopping or enjoying your iced latte.

A good and smart rule of thumb that will keep you and your dog safe on warm days: <u>never</u> leave them alone in your vehicle.
NOTE: also never leave your dog alone in a vehicle during cold weather because they can just as quickly suffer from hypothermia because your vehicle will turn into a large refrigerator during cold winter days just as quickly as it can turn into a deadly oven during the summer heat.

Chapter 15: Poisonous Foods & Plants

1. Poisonous Foods

While some dogs are smart enough not to want to eat foods that can harm or kill them, there are those canine companions that will eat absolutely anything they can get their teeth on, whether or not it's food.

If your dog is highly food motivated, in order to keep them safe and healthy, it will be very important to keep cupboards containing any food or poisonous products tightly closed and out of their reach. This will also include any area where you might store garbage because if they can smell it, they will figure out how to get to it.

As conscientious guardians for our furry friends, it will always be our responsibility to make certain that when we share our homes with a dog, we never leave foods (or other products) that could be toxic or lethal to them easily within their reach.

While there are many foods that can be toxic to a dog, the following alphabetical list contains some of the more common foods that can seriously harm or even kill our dogs including:

Bread Dough: if your dog eats bread dough, their body heat will cause the dough to rise inside the stomach. As the dough expands during the rising process, alcohol is produced.

Dogs who have eaten bread dough may experience stomach bloating, abdominal pain, vomiting, disorientation and depression. Because bread dough can rise to many times its original size, eating only a small amount will cause a problem for any dog.

Broccoli: the toxic ingredient in broccoli is isothiocynate. While it may cause stomach upset, it probably won't be very harmful unless the amount eaten is more than 10% of the dog's total daily diet.

Chocolate: contains theobromine, a chemical that is toxic to dogs in large enough quantities. Chocolate also contains caffeine, which is found in coffee, tea, and certain soft drinks. Different types of chocolate contain different amounts of theobromine and caffeine.

For example, dark chocolate and baking chocolate or cocoa powder contain more of these compounds than milk chocolate does, therefore, a dog would need to eat more milk chocolate in order to become ill.

However, even a few ounces of chocolate can be enough to cause illness or death in a puppy or smaller dog, therefore, no amount or type of chocolate should be considered safe for a dog to eat.

A dog suffering from having eaten chocolate may display symptoms that include diarrhea, vomiting, increased heart rate, restless behavior, muscle tremors, or seizures. If they have eaten enough of it, they could die within 24 hours of eating.

During many holidays such as Christmas, New Year's, Valentine's, Easter and Halloween, chocolate is often more easily accessible to curious dogs, especially from children who are not so careful with where they might keep their Halloween or Easter egg stash and who are an easy mark for a hungry dog.

In some cases, people unwittingly poison their dogs by offering them chocolate as a treat or leaving chocolate cookies or frosted cake easily within licking distance.

Caffeine: beverages containing caffeine, such as soda, tea, coffee, and chocolate, act as a stimulant and can accelerate your dog's heartbeat to a dangerous level. Dogs ingesting caffeine have been known to have seizures, some of which are fatal.

Cooked Bones: can be extremely hazardous for a dog because the bones become brittle when cooked which causes them to splinter when the dog chews on them.

The splinters have sharp edges that have been known to become stuck in the teeth, and cause choking when caught in the throat or create a rupture or puncture of the stomach lining or intestinal tract.

Especially dangerous are cooked turkey and chicken legs, ham, pork chop and veal bones. Symptoms of choking include:
- Pale or blue gums
- Gasping breathing or panting
- Pawing or scratching at the face
- Slowed, shallow breathing
- Collapse and unconsciousness with dilated pupils

Grapes and Raisins: can cause acute (sudden) kidney failure in dogs. While it is not known what the toxic agent is in this fruit, clinical signs can occur within 24 hours of eating and include vomiting, diarrhea, and lethargy (tiredness). Other signs of illness caused from eating grapes or raisins relate to the eventual shutdown of kidney functioning.

Garlic and Onions: contain chemicals that damage red blood cells by rupturing them so that they lose their ability to carry oxygen effectively, which leave the dog short of oxygen, causing what is called *"hemolytic anemia"*.

Poisoning can occur when a dog eats a large amount of garlic or onions all at once, or when eating repeated meals containing smaller amounts and cooking does not reduce the potential toxicity of onions and garlic.

NOTE: fresh, cooked, and/or powdered garlic or onions are commonly found in baby food, which is sometimes given to dogs when they are sick, therefore, be certain to carefully read food labels before feeding to your Beabull.

Macadamia Nuts: are commonly found in candies and chocolates. Although the mechanism of macadamia nut toxicity is not well understood, the clinical signs in dogs having eaten these nuts include depression, weakness, vomiting, tremors, joint pain, and pale gums.

Signs can occur within 12 hours after eating. In some cases, symptoms can resolve themselves without treatment within 24 to 48 hours. However, keeping a close eye on your Beabull will be strongly recommended.

Mushrooms: mushroom poisoning can be fatal if certain species of mushrooms are eaten.

The most commonly reported severely toxic species of mushroom in the US is Amanita phalloides (Death Cap mushroom), which is also quite a common species found in most parts of Britain. Other Amanita species are also toxic. This deadly mushroom is often found growing in grassy or wooded areas near various deciduous and coniferous trees, which mean that if you're out walking with your dog in the woods, they could easily find these mushrooms.

Eating them can cause severe liver disease and neurological disorders. If you suspect your dog has eaten these mushrooms, immediately take them to your veterinarian, as the recommended treatment is to induce vomiting and to give activated charcoal. Further treatment for liver disease may also be necessary.

Pits and Seeds: many seeds and pits found in a variety of fruits, including apples, apricots, cherries, pears and plums, contain cyanogenic glycosides that can cause cyanide poisoning in your dog.

The symptoms of cyanide poisoning usually occur within 15-20 minutes to a few hours after eating and symptoms can include initial excitement, followed by rapid respiration rate, salivation or drooling, voiding of urine and feces, vomiting, muscle spasm, staggering, and coma before death.

Dogs suffering from cyanide poisoning that live more than 2 hours after onset of symptoms will usually recover.

Raw Salmon or Trout: Salmon Poisoning Disease (SPD) can be a problem for anyone who goes fishing with their dog, or feeds their dog a raw meat diet that includes raw salmon or trout.

When a snail is infected and then is eaten by the fish as part of the food chain, the dog is exposed when it eats the infected fish. A sudden onset of symptoms can occur 5-7 days after eating the infected fish. In the acute stages, gastrointestinal symptoms are quite similar to canine parvovirus.

SPD has a mortality rate of up to 90%, can be diagnosed with a fecal sample and is treatable if caught in time. Prevention is simple, cook all fish before feeding it to your dog and immediately see your veterinarian if you suspect that your dog has eaten raw salmon or trout.

Tobacco: all forms of tobacco, including patches, nicotine gum and chewing tobacco can be fatal to dogs if eaten. Signs of poisoning can appear quite rapidly (within an hour or less) and may include diarrhea, vomiting, a heightened state of activity, excessive drooling and panting.

Depending upon how much a dog may have eaten, more acute signs of poisoning may cause twitching, leading to collapse and coma due to heart attack that will cause death.

Never leave tobacco products within reach of your puppy or dog, and be careful not to let them pick up discarded cigarette butts when they are young puppies. If you suspect your dog has eaten cigarette butts, seek immediate veterinary help.

TIP: when your dog is a very young puppy, use a double leash, collar and harness arrangement, so that you can still teach them to walk on leash with a Martingale collar around their neck, but can also attach the second leash to their harness so that you can easily lift them over enticing cigarette butts or other toxic garbage they may be trying to eat during your walks.

Tomatoes: tomatoes contain a substance called atropine, which can cause tremors, dilated pupils and an irregular heartbeat in a puppy or dog that eats them. The greatest amount of atropine will be found in the stalks and leaves of the tomato plant, next is the green tomato (before it ripens), and then ripe tomatoes.

Xylitol: is an artificial sweetener often found in many candies, gums, breath mints, toothpastes and mouthwashes that is recognized by the National Animal Poison Control Center to be a poison risk to dogs.

When puppies or dogs eat products containing Xylitol, it causes a sudden release of insulin, which in turn causes low blood sugar, which can also cause liver damage.

Within 30 minutes after eating a product containing Xylitol, the dog may vomit, be lethargic (tired), and/or be uncoordinated. However, some signs of toxicity can also be delayed for hours or even for a few days. Xylitol toxicity in dogs can be fatal if left untreated.

Please be aware that the above list is just some of the more common foods that can be toxic or fatal to our fur friends and that there are many other foods we should never be feeding our dogs.

If you have one of those dogs who will happily eat anything that looks or smells even slightly like food, or even if not food, but is enticing for a puppy or dog to eat, be certain to keep these foods or products far away from your beloved Beabull and you'll help them to live a long and healthy life.

2. Poisonous Household Plants

Many common house plants are actually poisonous to our canine companions, and although many dogs simply will ignore house plants, some will attempt to eat anything, especially puppies who want to taste everything in their new world.

More than 700 plant species contain toxins that may harm or be fatal to puppies or dogs, depending on the size of the puppy or dog and how much they may eat. Therefore, it is especially important to be aware of household plants that could be toxic when you are sharing your home with a new puppy.

Following is a short list of the more common household plants, what they look like, the different names they are known by, and what symptoms might be apparent if your puppy or dog decides to eat them.

Aloe Plant: also known as *"medicine plant or Barbados aloe",* is a very common succulent plant that is toxic to dogs.

Asparagus Fern: is also known as *"lace fern, emerald fern, emerald feather, sprengeri fern and plumosa fern".*

Corn Plant: also known as *"ribbon plant, cornstalk plant, dragon tree and dracaena",* is toxic to dogs.

Cyclamen: also known as *"Sowbread"*, is a pretty, flowering plant that, if eaten, can cause diarrhea, vomiting and increased salivation.

Dieffenbachia: also known as *"exotica, dumb cane and tropic snow"* contains a chemical that is a poisonous deterrent to animals.

Elephant Ear: also known as *"cape, caladium, malanga, pai, taro and via sori,"* contains a chemical which is similar to a chemical also found in dieffenbachia.

Heartleaf Philodendron: also known as "cordatum, split-leaf philodendron, fiddle leaf, fruit salad plant, horsehead philodendron, panda plant, red emerald, red princess, and saddle leaf", is a very common, easy-to-grow houseplant that contains a chemical irritating to the mouth, tongue and lips of dogs.

Jade Plant: has many other names, including "baby jade, Chinese rubber plant, dwarf rubber plant, friendship tree, jade tree, or Japanese rubber plant".

Lilies: some plants of the lily family can be toxic to dogs. The peace lily (also known as Mauna Loa) is known to be toxic to dogs.

Satin Pothos: (silk pothos), if eaten by a dog, the plant may cause irritation to the dog's mouth, lips and tongue, while the dog may also experience vomiting, difficulty swallowing and drooling.

The plants noted above are only a few of the more common household plants, and every conscientious Dog guardian will want to educate themselves before bringing plants into the home that could be toxic to their canine companions.

3. Poison Proof Your Home

You can learn about many potentially toxic and poisonous sources both inside and outside your home by visiting the ASPCA Animal Poison Control Center website. Always keep your veterinarian's emergency number in a place where you can quickly access it, as well as the Emergency Poison Control telephone number, in case you suspect that your dog may have been poisoned.

Knowing what to do if you suspect your dog may have been poisoned and being able to quickly contact the right people could save your dog's life.

If you keep toxic cleaning substances (including fertilizers, vermin or snail poisons and vehicle products) in your home, garage or garden shed, always keep them behind closed doors. As well, keep any medications where your dog can never get to them, and seriously consider eliminating the use of any and all toxic products, for the health of both yourself, your family and your best fur friends.

4. Garden Plants

Please note that there are also many outdoor plants that can be toxic or poisonous to your puppy or dog, therefore, always check what plants are growing in your garden and if any may be harmful, remove them or make certain that your puppy or adult dog cannot eat them.

Cornell University, Department of Animal Science lists many different categories of poisonous plants affecting dogs, including:

- house plants
- flower garden plants
- vegetable garden plants
- plants found in swamps or moist areas
- plants found in fields, trees and shrubs
- plants found in wooded areas
- ornamental plants

5. Why Does My Dog Eat Grass?

Be aware that many puppies and adult dogs will eat grass, just because.

Perhaps they are curious, bored, or need a little fiber in their diet. Remember that canines are natural scavengers always on the look out for something they can eat, and so long as the grass is healthy and has not been sprayed with toxic chemicals, a little grass eating should not be a concern.

6. Animal Poison Control Centers

The ASPCA Animal Poison Control Center is staffed 24 hours a day, 365 days a year and is a valuable resource for learning about what plants are toxic and possibly poisonous to your dog.

ASPCA Poison Control: www.aspca.org

a) USA Poison Emergency: **Call: 1 (888) 426-4435**

When calling the Poison Emergency number, your credit card may be charged with a $65. ((£49.42) consultation fee.

b) UK Poison Emergency: Call: 0800-213-6680 - Pet Poison Helpline (payable service)

RSPCA: Call: 0300 1234 999

Chapter 16: Caring for Aging Dogs

1. What to Be Aware Of

As a result of many modern advances in veterinarian care, improvements in diet and nutrition and general knowledge concerning proper care of our canine companions, our dogs are able to enjoy longer, healthier lives.

As such, when caring for our canine companions, we need to be aware of behavioral and physical changes that will affect our dogs as they approach old age. While each dog's individual health, genetics, and spirit will affect how old they seem, and they may remain quite as they get older active, a Beabull will be entering their senior years at around 8 to 10 years of age.

a) Physiological Changes: as our beloved canine companions enter into their senior years, they may be suffering from very similar physical aging problems that affect us humans, such as pain, stiffness and arthritis, and inability to control their bowels and bladder. Any of these problems will reduce a dog's willingness to want to exercise.

b) Behavioral Changes: a senior Beabull may experience behavioral changes resulting from loss of hearing and sight, such as disorientation, fear or startle reactions and overall grumpiness from any number of physical problems that could be causing them pain whenever they move.

Just as research and science has improved our human quality of life in our senior years, the same is becoming true for our canine counterparts who are able to benefit from dietary supplements and pharmaceutical products to help them be as comfortable as possible in their senior years.

Of course, there will be some inconveniences associated with keeping a dog with advancing years around the home, however, your Beabull deserves no less than to spend their final days in your loving care after they have unconditionally given you their entire lives.

c) Geriatric Dogs: being aware of the changes that are likely occurring in a senior dog will help you to better care for them during their geriatric years. For instance, most dogs will experience hearing loss and visual impairment, and how you help them will depend upon which goes first (hearing or sight).

If a dog's hearing is compromised, then using more hand signals will be helpful. Deaf dogs will still be able to hear louder noises and feel vibrations, therefore hand clapping, knocking on walls, doors or furniture, using a loud clicker or stomping your foot on the floor may be a way to get their attention.

If a senior dog loses their eyesight, most dogs will still be able to easily navigate their familiar surroundings, and you will only need to be extra watchful on their behalf when taking them to unfamiliar territory.

If they still have their hearing, you will be able to assist your dog with verbal cues and commands. Dogs that have lost both their hearing and their sight will need to be close to you so that they can relax and not feel nervous, and so that you can communicate by touching parts of their body.

Generally speaking, even when a dog becomes blind and/or deaf, their powerful sense of smell is still functioning, which means that they will be able to smell where you are and navigate their environment by using their nose.

d) More Bathroom Breaks: bathroom breaks may need to become more frequent in older dogs who may lose their ability to hold it for longer periods of time, so be prepared to be more watchful and to offer them opportunities to go outside more frequently during the day.

You may also want to place a pee pad near the door, in case they just can't hold it long enough, or if you have not already taught them to go to the bathroom on an indoor potty patch, or pee pad, now may be the time for this alternative bathroom arrangement.

A dog who has been house trained for years will feel the shame and upset of not being able to hold it long enough to get to their regular bathroom location, so be kind and do whatever you need to do in order to help them not to have to feel bad about failing bowel or bladder control.

Our beloved canine companions may also begin to show signs of cognitive decline and changes in the way their brain functions, similar to what happens to humans suffering from Alzheimer's, where they start to wander about aimlessly, sometimes during the middle of the night. If your senior dog is wandering at night, make sure that they cannot accidentally fall down stairs or harm themselves in any way.

Being aware that an aging Beabull will be experiencing many symptoms that are similar to an aging human will help you to understand how best to keep them safe and as comfortable as possible during this golden time in their lives.

2. How to Make Them Comfortable

1) Regular Checkups: during this time in your dog's life, when their immune systems become weakened and they may be experiencing pain, you will want to get into the habit of taking your senior dog for regular veterinarian checkups.

Take them for a checkup every six months so that early detection of any problems can quickly be attended to and solutions for helping to keep your aging dog comfortable can be provided.

2) No Rough Play: an older Beabull will not have the same energy or willingness to play that they did when they were younger, therefore, do not allow younger children to rough house with an older dog. Explain to them that the dog is getting older and that as a result they must learn to be gentle and to leave the dog alone when it may want to rest or sleep.

3) Mild Exercise: dogs still love going for walks, even when they are getting older and slowing down. Although an older Beabull will generally have less energy, they still need to exercise and keep moving, and taking them out regularly for shorter or slower walks will keep them healthier and happier long into old age.

4) Best Quality Food: everyone has heard the saying, *"you are what you eat"* and for a senior dog, what he or she eats is even more important as his or her digestive system may no longer be functioning at peak performance. Therefore, feeding a high quality, protein-based food will be important for a senior dog's continued health.

As well, if your older Beabull is overweight, you will want to help them shed excess pounds so that they will not be placing undue stress on their joints or heart, and the best way to accomplish this is by feeding smaller quantities of a higher quality food.

5) Clean and Parasite Free: the last thing an aging dog should have to suffer is the misery of itching and scratching. Make sure that you continue to give them regular baths with the appropriate shampoos and conditioners to keep their coat and skin comfortable and free from biting bugs.

6) Plenty of Water: proper hydration is essential for helping to keep an older Beabull comfortable. Water is life giving for every creature, so make certain that your aging dog has easy access to plenty of clean, fresh water which will help to improve their energy and digestion and also prevent dehydration which can add to joint stiffness.

7) Keep Them Warm: just as older humans feel the cold more, so do older dogs. Keeping your senior dog warm will help to alleviate some of the pain of their joint stiffness or arthritis.

Make sure their bed or kennel is not kept in a drafty location and perhaps consider a heated bed for them. Aging dog are often more sensitive to extremes in temperature, and it will be up to you to make sure that they are comfortable at all times, which means not too hot and not too cold.

8) Indoor Clothing: we humans tend to wear warmer clothing as we get older, simply because we have more difficulty maintaining a comfortable body temperature and the same will be true of our senior canine companions.

Therefore, if your older dog has thinning hair, now may be the time to consider canine clothing appropriate to the climate in which you live. You could consider doggy t-shirts or sweater clothing options to help keep your aging companion comfortably warm when inside the home.

9) Steps or Stairs: if your dog is allowed to sleep on the human couch or chair, but they are having difficulties getting up there as their joints are becoming stiff and painful, consider buying or making them a set of soft, foam stairs so that they do not have to make the jump to their favorite sleeping place.

10) Comfortable Bed: while most dogs seem to be happy with sleeping on the floor, providing a padded, soft bed will greatly help to relieve sore spots and joint pain in older dogs. If there is a draft in the home, generally it will be at floor level, therefore, a bed that is raised up off of the floor will be warmer for your senior fur friend.

11) More Love and Attention: make sure that your senior dog receives lots of love and attention and never leave them alone for long periods of time. When they are not feeling their best, they will want to be with you all that much more because you are their trusted guardian whom they love beyond life itself.

3. What is Euthanasia?

Every veterinarian will have received special training to help provide all incurably ill, injured or aged pets that have come to the end of their natural lives with a humane and gentle death, through a process called *"euthanasia"*. When the time comes, euthanasia, or putting a dog *"to sleep"*, will usually be a two-step process.

First, the veterinarian will inject the dog with a sedative to make them sleepy, calm and comfortable. Second, the veterinarian will inject a special drug that will peacefully stop their heart.

These drugs work in such a way that the dog will not experience any awareness whatsoever that his or her life is transitioning toward a peaceful ending. What they will experience is very much like what we humans experience when falling asleep under anesthesia during a surgical procedure.

Once the second stage drug has been injected, the entire process takes about 10 to 20 seconds, at which time the veterinarian will then check to make certain that the dog's heart has stopped. There is no suffering with this process, which is a very gentle and humane way to end a dog's suffering and allow them to peacefully pass on.

4. When to Help a Dog Transition

The impending loss of a beloved dog is one of the most painfully difficult and emotionally devastating experiences a canine guardian will ever have to face. For the sake of our faithful companions, because we do not want to prolong their suffering, we humans will have to do our best to look at our dog's situation practically, rather than emotionally, so that we can make the best decision for them.

They may be suffering from extreme old age and the inability to even walk outside to relieve themselves, and thus having to deal with the indignity of regularly soiling their sleeping area, they may have been diagnosed with an incurable illness that is causing them much pain, or they may have been seriously injured.

Whatever the reason for a canine companion's suffering, it will be up to their human guardian to calmly guide the end-of-life experience so that any further discomfort and distress can be minimized.

5. What to Do If You Are Uncertain

In circumstances where it is not entirely clear how much a dog is suffering, it will be helpful to pay close attention to your dog's behavior and keep a daily log or record so that you can know for certain how much of their day is difficult and painful for them, and how much is not.

When you keep a daily log, it will be easier to decide if the dog's quality of life has become so poor that it makes better sense to offer them the gift of peacefully going to sleep.

During this time of uncertainty, it will also be very important to discuss with your veterinarian what signs of suffering may be associated with the dog's particular disease or condition, so that you know what to look for.

Often a dog may still continue to eat or drink despite being upset, having difficulty breathing, excessively panting, being disoriented or in much pain, and as their caring guardians, we will have to weigh their love of eating against how much they are really suffering in all other aspects of their life.

Obviously, if a canine guardian can clearly see that their beloved companion is suffering throughout their days and nights, it will make sense to help humanely end their suffering by planning a euthanasia procedure.

We humans are often tempted to delay the inevitable moment of euthanasia, because we love our dogs so much and cannot bear the anticipation of the intense grief we know will overwhelm us when we must say our final goodbyes to our beloved fur friend.

Unfortunately, we may regret that we allowed our dog to suffer too long, and could find ourselves wishing that if only we humans had the same option, to peacefully let go, when in our own lives, we find ourselves in such a position.

6. Grieving a Lost Friend

Some humans do not fully recognize the terrible grief involved in losing a beloved canine friend. There will be many who do not understand the close bond we humans can have with our dogs, which is often unlike any we have with our human counterparts.

Your friends may give you pitying looks and try to cheer you up, but if they have never experienced such a loss themselves, they may also secretly think that you are making too much fuss over "just a dog".

For some of us humans, the loss of a beloved dog is so painful that we decide never to share our lives with another, because we cannot bear the thought of going through the pain of loss again.

Expect to feel terribly sad, tearful and yes, depressed because those who are close to their canine companions will feel their loss no less acutely than the loss of a human friend or life partner. The grieving process can take some time to recover from, and some of us never totally recover.

After the loss of a family dog, first you need to take care of yourself by making certain that you keep eating and getting regular sleep, even though you will feel an almost eerie sense of loneliness.

Losing a beloved dog is a serious shock to the system, which can also affect your concentration and your ability to find joy or want to participate in other activities that may be part of your daily life.

During this early grieving time you will need to take extra care while driving or performing tasks that require your concentration as you may find yourself distracted.

If there are other dogs or pets in the home, they will also be grieving the loss of a companion, and may display this by acting depressed, being off their food or showing little interest in play or games. Therefore, you need to help guide your other pets through this grieving process by keeping them busy and interested, taking them for extra walks and spending more time with them.

Many people do not wait long enough before attempting to replace a lost pet and will immediately go to the local shelter and rescue a deserving dog. While this may help to distract you from your grieving process, this is not really fair to the new fur member of your family.

Bringing a new pet into a home that is depressed and grieving the loss of a long time canine member may create behavioral problems for the new dog who will be faced with learning all about their new home while also dealing with the unstable, sad energy of the grieving family.

A better scenario would be to allow yourself the time to properly grieve by waiting a minimum of one month to allow yourself and your family to feel happier and have more stable energy before deciding upon sharing your home with another dog.

The grieving process will be different for everyone and you will know when the time is right to consider sharing your home with another canine companion.

7. The Rainbow Bridge Poem

"Just this side of heaven is a
place called Rainbow Bridge.
When an animal dies that has been
especially close to someone here,
that pet goes to Rainbow Bridge.
There are meadows and hills for all of our special friends
so they can run and play together.
There is plenty of food, water and sunshine,
and our friends are warm and comfortable.

All the animals who had been ill and old
are restored to health and vigor;
those who were hurt or maimed
are made whole and strong again,
just as we remember them in our dreams
of days and times gone by.
The animals are happy and content,
except for one small thing;
they each miss someone very special to them,
who had to be left behind.

They all run and play together,
but the day comes when one suddenly stops
and looks into the distance.
His bright eyes are intent; His eager body quivers.
Suddenly he begins to run from the group,
flying over the green grass,
his legs carrying him faster and faster.

You have been spotted,
and when you and your special friend finally meet,
you cling together in joyous reunion,
never to be parted again.
The happy kisses rain upon your face;
your hands again caress the beloved head,
and you look once more into the trusting eyes

of your pet, so long gone from your life
but never absent from your heart.

Then you cross Rainbow Bridge together...."

~Author unknown~

8. Memorials

There are as many ways to honor the passing of a beloved pet, as each of our furry friends is uniquely special to us. For instance, you and your family may wish to have your companion cremated and preserve their ashes in a special urn or sprinkle their ashes along their favorite walk, across the lake where they loved to swim, or perhaps turn his or her precious ashes into a diamond that lasts forever at Eterneva.com.

Perhaps you will want to have a special marker, photo bereavement, photo engraved Rainbow Bridge Poem, or wooden plaque created in honor of your passed friend, or you may wish to keep their memory close to you at all times by having a DNA remembrance pendant or bracelet designed.

For instance, a wonderful way to commemorate the passing of a beloved companion may be by wearing a unique bracelet or necklace that wordlessly symbolizes the close relationship we have with our dogs and helps to support dogs in need all at the same time, or you might want to engage the services of a wildlife artist to paint a picture in remembrance of your beloved companion.

Volunteering at a shelter or rescue facility to help homeless dogs can also help to ease the pain of losing your best friend.

There are many ways to remember and honor the passing of a wonderful fur friend and you will need to find the one that means the most to you.

As well, there are support groups, such as Rainbow Bridge, which is a grief support community, to help you and your family through this painful period of loss and grief.

"Dogs make humans feel special."
~Asia Moore~

Chapter 17: Rescue Organizations

When you are considering rescuing a specific breed of dog or puppy, the first place to start your search will be with your local breeders, shelters and rescue groups.

There are many breed specific rescue organizations in Canada, the USA, the United Kingdom and many other countries and the easiest way to find one closest to you is to go online and type in the breed name of the dog you want to rescue next to the name of the city where you live. As well, if you have the free Dogalize app on your smart device, you will be able to easily search for rescues in your specific area and see pictures of available dogs.

1. Shelters
Here you can expect to pay an adoption fee to cover the cost of spaying or neutering, but this will be only a small percentage of what you would pay a breeder, and you will be saving a life at the same time.

2. Online Resources
Sites such as Petango, Adopt A Pet and Pet Finder can be good places to begin your search. Each of these online resources is a central gathering site for hundreds and hundreds of local shelters, humane societies and rescue groups.

3. Canine Clubs and Breeders
Another place to search will be hybrid clubs or breeders in your local area. These groups may have rescue dogs available.

Chapter 18: Resources & References

NOTE: at the time of printing, all the websites below were working. As the Internet changes rapidly, some sites might no longer be live when you read this book, which is, of course, out of our control.

1. Poison Control

ASPCA Poison Control: www.aspca.org
Poisonous Plants Affecting Dogs - Cornell University, Department of Animal Science
www.ansi.cornell.edu/plants/dogs/

2. Breeders, Registries, Rescues & More

Adopt A Pet: www.adoptapet.com
Designer Dogs – The Kennel Club: www.thekennelclub.org.uk
Free Ads: www.freeads.co.uk
Merry's Bullies: www.merrybullies.com
National Dog Tattoo Register: www.dog-register.co.uk
National Dog Registry: www.nationaldogregistry.com
Petango: www.petango.com
Pet Finder: www.petfinder.com
Pets 4 Homes: www.pets4homes.co.uk
Smith's Unparalleled Bullies: www.smiths-beabulls.com
The American Canine Hybrid Club: www.achclub.com
The International Designer Canine Registry:
www.designercanineregistry.com
The National Hybrid Registry: www.nationalhybridregistry.com

3. Equipment, Supplies & Services

Dog Bowl for Your Dog: www.dogbowlforyourdog.com
Eterneva: www.eterneva.com
Mim VarioCage: www.mightymitedoggear.com
Modern Puppies: www.modernpuppies.com
Potty Patch: www.pottypatch.com
Remove Urine Odors: www.removeurineodors.com
Tell Bell™: www.tellbell.com

4. Memorials

Rainbow Bridge: www.rainbowbridge.com

Published by Zoodoo Publishing 2021

www.ingramcontent.com/pod-product-compliance
Lightning Source LLC
Chambersburg PA
CBHW052002090426
42741CB00008B/1517